LORRIES, TRUCKS AND VANS
1927 -1973

ARTHUR INGRAM

BLANDFORD PRESS

First published in 1975
© 1975 Blandford Press Ltd
Link House, West Street, Poole, Dorset BH15 1LL

ISBN 0 7137 0732 1

Colour printed in Great Britain by
Colour Reproductions, Billericay
Text printed and books bound by Tinling (1973) *Ltd*

CONTENTS

ACKNOWLEDGMENTS
AND BIBLIOGRAPHY

The author would like to thank all the firms and organisations which rendered assistance with regard to this volume, and in particular the following individuals who have helped with illustrations and information: Larry Auten, Sven Bengtson, Peter Davies, Brad Dunkin, Bryan Edwards, Nick Georgano, Ron Gooch, G L Hartner, Prince Marshall, Colin Peck, Martin Phippard, and Bart Vanderveen.

Much of the information on old trucks comes from brochures, magazines and books published in the past. There has been little published in book form concerning the commercial vehicle and a short list of some useful titles is given below for those desiring further reading on the subject.

PERIODICALS

AEC Gazette (now ceased publication) London
American Automobile New York
Commercial Motor London
Commercial Vehicle Users Journal (later *Commercial Vehicles*, both now ceased publication) London
Leyland Journal (now ceased publication) Leyland
Motor Transport London
Move Magazine published by the CVRTC, see below
Old Motor Magazine published by the OM CLUB, see below
Truck and Bus Sydney
Worlds Carriers (now ceased publication) London

BOOKS

British Lorries, C F Klapper, London, 1973

Commercial Road Vehicles, E L Cornwell, London, 1960

Commercial Vehicles of the World, J F J Kuipers, Lingfield, 1972

Development of the English Steam Wagon, R H Clark, Norwich 1963

Dumpy Book of Motors and Road Transport, H Sampson, London, 1957

Dumpy Pocketbook of Cars and Commercial Vehicles, R A Orr, London, 1960

Mack, John Montville, New York, 1973

Observer's Book of Commercial Vehicles, L A Manwaring, London, 1966

Observer's Book of Commercial Vehicles, Olyslager Organisation, London, 1971

Observer's Fighting Vehicles Directory, B H Vanderveen, London, 1972

Relics of the Road GMC, Gini Rice, New York, 1973

Relics of the Road Kenworth, Gini Rice, New York, 1973

Source Book of Commercial Vehicles, Olyslager Organisation, London, 1973

The World's Commercial Vehicles, G N Georgano, London, 1965

CVRTC 50 The Firs, Daventry, Northamptonshire.

Old Motor Club, 17 Air Street, London W1.

ABBREVIATIONS

hp	rated horsepower
bhp	brake horsepower
gvw	gross vehicle weight
gtw	gross train weight (vehicle+trailer)
gcw	gross combination weight (articulated vehicle)
coe	cab over engine
fc	forward control (flat fronted cab)
nc	normal control (bonneted type)
rpm	revolutions per minute

PREFACE

This book is a companion to Volume I of the same title which covered the period up to 1927. This arbitrary date was chosen because by that time the commercial vehicle had progressed to such an extent as to be a respectable piece of engineering design which paid due regard to comfort, speed and cost.

This second volume attempts to trace the subsequent history of the commercial from the end of 1927 through periods of depression, competition, war, recovery, expansion and rationalisation. All the time there has been an underlying basis of progress in design and engineering accomplishment which has made the commercial vehicle industry one of the most important in the world today.

Recently it has become fashionable to hurl abuse at the lorry. Many writers and speakers who should better understand the reasons for its existence talk of juggernauts and want all the goods traffic carried by rail. One can just imagine railway lines down every street so that the milk delivery or the furniture removal can be done by railways! Anyway, who said that roads were reserved for cars and bicycles?

Why goods should go by rail and persons should have priority by road is difficult to understand. As the facility of movement from door to door is completely unobtainable by rail, and therefore every item has to be handled in some way or another, it would seem logical that until every factory, dock, warehouse, shop and house is rail connected then goods will have to be moved by road.

On the other hand as passengers have their own inbuilt system of locomotion suitable for short distances it is not unreasonable that they should be guided from house, office, factory and holiday resort to the railway facilities for their longer journeys.

Another disturbing factor in the anti-lorry campaign which is not mentioned is the fact that railway operators are among the largest users of road vehicles, and that these are almost without exception goods carrying vehicles! Yet how many road transport operators can boast their own railway system? Here is a sure indication that the lorry is accepted as necessary.

As someone once said, 'transport is civilisation' and without a speedy, cheap, reliable and flexible transport system the modern economy would surely come to a halt. Roads provide that system and lorries deliver the goods.

So readers will notice that the text is to a large extent transport orientated, that is to say not merely a list of technical notes on the first chassis produced by XYZ, or the largest, or the heaviest, etc., etc. Commercial vehicles are produced for a purpose – work, and to show them in museum-like isolationism is to remove their very soul. The complete vehicles are illustrated in most cases because often the bodywork is just as important as the chassis which it surmounts, although many writers tend to ignore the body.

Another facet of the story which needs clarification is that relating to military vehicles. A whole torrent of material has appeared in recent years dealing with the military vehicle and its place in modern warfare, while just a trickle has been written on the less glamorous civilian counterpart. In this volume there is scant reference to purely war vehicles as they are adequately chronicled elsewhere.

In the Plate descriptions the technical notes are recorded as found in the various references studied. On the continent of Europe the metric system is supreme while North America clings to pounds and inches. In Britain we have that peculiar mixture with some specifications culled in Imperial terms while others favour the metric system for things technical. With regard to cylinder dimensions, these are arranged as bore and stroke no matter to what standard of measurement.

Other shortened terms are given on page 8.

No doubt errors and omissions have crept in and these are regretted. The colour schemes have been checked as far as is possible with old records and memories, but not all references survive. To those who do not see their particular favourite illustrated, I am sorry, but in a volume of this size it is impossible to show them all. Anyway, I do have a few special types of my own choice and no doubt some friends will recognise these!

Where wheel arrangements are given thus: 4×4, 6×2, the first figure represents the number of wheels on the vehicle with twin tyres counted as one wheel, and the second refers to the number of driven or powered wheels.

INTRODUCTION

The commercial vehicle industry of the world, like many other industries, has always tried to woo prospective customers by the frequent introduction of new or improved models at regular intervals. The showpiece for such developments has always been the various National and International motor shows which have been presented in many capitals of the world almost since the inception of the motor vehicle.

In London, Paris, Berlin, Brussels, Geneva and Chicago the heavy motor industry and its distributor networks have shown to the world the latest models, designs and productions. Although this less glamorous part of such a vital industry has in the past always been geared to attracting the industrial user, in recent years the publicity machine has made some of the heavy vehicles almost as attractive as their lighter relations.

This volume really begins toward the end of 1927 when the wrappers were taken off the 1928 models. As events later proved this was to mark the beginning of a particularly interesting and important period in commercial vehicle development.

Many improvements and innovations came to light during the ensuing years including six wheelers and six cylinder engines, giant pneumatics, low loading chassis, lightweight materials, insulated bodies, demountable containers, instantaneous couplings, large articulated vehicles, larger trailers, eight wheel chassis, the demise of the steamer and the widespread acceptance of the oiler. Electrics had a great revival; there were new small vans specially designed for multi-stop operations. Stainless steel came into use for bodies, while there were more refrigerated bodies, tail lifts, tilt cabs and bulk powder tankers. Other innovations included tubeless tyres, alternators, electric retarders, bonded brake linings, air brakes, multi speed gearboxes, powered trailers, anti-jack-knife devices, the increasing use of liquified petroleum gas and gas turbines, and a whole host of others.

Unfortunately the era also saw some casualties in the ranks of the makers because of financial and other pressures. At the beginning of the period the tremendous slump in trade dealt a severe blow to many small firms and legislation also hampered the natural progress of design and ideas.

In Britain, France, Germany and the United States national or local state controls and regulations were all seemingly aimed at stifling expansion in the road section of land transport. In Europe, America, Australia and South Africa the pressure was being put on the road transport operator, who was blamed for the loss of rail traffic. In some spheres higher taxation and more stringent regulations concerning construction and use made things more difficult for both producer and user. In other places licensing of operators and their vehicles was being used as a means of 'regulating' the amount of transport available. This took the form of limits on number of vehicles, size of vehicle or area of operation. Another means of control was by a system of co-operation with rail interests so that only local transport was carried on and the road vehicle merely acted as a feeder for rail services.

In Germany a very different situation developed. With its head start in diesel engine development it was only natural that the motor industry of the Fatherland should maintain its lead in production figures. So in the period 1928–32 many German vehicle builders were going ahead with the oil engine·as the power unit of the future. Naturally it was firms such as Benz, Bussing, MAN, Krupp, Henchel and Junkers who had the resources to continue through this difficult period when some of the others were falling by the wayside.

Competition was fierce and some thought that import tariffs were too low thus allowing the importation of vehicles which undermined the home industry. There was considerable un-employment and the German government was urging manu-facturers to develop engines capable of running on a mixture of petrol and home produced alcohol or producer gas. They were not alone in this: both France and Belgium, and to a lesser extent Britain, were busy exploring the possibilities of alternative fuels and mobile gas generators.

The one bright spot in all the gloom was the German national-istic pride in making the country efficient, busy and forward looking. To this end everyone was being urged to improve output and get the country back on its feet. Almost overnight new legi-slation was passed setting up trade associations, and a railway subsidiary was created to administer the building of a high speed motor road network. The motor industry rallied quickly by increasing their work force and planning vehicles capable of taking advantage of the proposed new *autobahnen*. Vehicle production went up and soon an army of 150,000 labourers were busy on the new road.

While the 1929 Berlin Show had been cancelled, allegedly because of the fear of too much foreign competition, in 1934–35 Herr Hitler was urging far more frequent shows in order to publicise the expanding industry. Mercedes Benz, Bussing, Henschel and Krupp responded with some enormous vehicles ready for new high speed long distance routes. These designs were really the progenitors of the many international haulage vehicles of future years, with the lorry and trailer outfit handling the bulk of the traffic up until quite recently when 'artics' have established themselves. At the time of writing the drawbar trailer is enjoying a comeback, and there are signs that this trend will continue unless there are pressures from outside by way of legislation against it.

Returning to the Berlin Show for a moment it is worth recording that Henschel actually went as far as producing a new steam wagon during the mid thirties, no doubt to show that they were trying to avoid the use of imported fuel! This was a design of flash boiler operating at 1,500 lbs per sq in. on the Doble principle with engine geared direct to the driving axle.

Another feature of this era was the use of road tractors with Germany, France and Britain all using them for towing either one or two trailers at slow speeds. Makers included Kaelble and Hanomag in Germany, Chenard Walcker and Latil in France and Fordson, International, Latil and Beardmore in Britain.

For really heavy traction jobs the steamer was being eclipsed by heavy petrol and oil engined tractors. The tonnage moved was going up almost every month as larger boilers, castings, locomotives, transformers, and so on were moved about.

The diesel engine had been the product of Germany and Switzerland during the 1920's but it was not until the thirties that it came into use in very great numbers. Its use spread throughout the countries of Europe quite quickly but it did not penetrate America to the same extent during this period although several truck makers offered it as optional or standard equipment.

In the period leading up to World War II the situation was more difficult than might be apparent in retrospect. The depression years left their mark on the ranks of the vehicle builders and some suffered through trying just too hard to please everybody. The way some firms offered a different model for every half ton of payload from about 15 cwt to 5 tons was hardly economical. Then came war preparation with shortages of everything. Viewed by some as the salvation of some companies who were engaged on war production, these years certainly left their mark on vehicle design and production methods.

The postwar years with their shortages of new vehicles gave some small builders a start in life with some prospering and others later fading from the scene. Demand for vehicles continued with the rebuilding of towns and industry, the growth of developing countries and the making of agreements for building vehicles at plants overseas. Exports have always been essential to European countries and the commercial vehicle industry has certainly played its part in that market.

In recent years alternatives to the oil engine have been mooted with liquefied petroleum gas and the gas turbine getting their due publicity. Gross weights have been increased while trends toward weight saving continue to be pursued. More attention has been given to better roads of adequate capacity in order to accommodate the increasing number of vehicles in use and the environmentalists have had their say concerning noise, vibration, size, weights and parking.

Looking to the future we shall probably have quieter, sweeter smelling lorries with greater restrictions on area of use. No doubt heavier gross weights will follow but possibly spread over more axles and tyres with restrictions as to routes and with much greater use of terminals for breaking of bulk. The container or demountable body fits in with this concept quite well.

BROCKWAY
[1]

Brockway had their beginnings as carriage builders, but in 1912 the Brockway Motor Truck Company was formed. Many Brockway trucks saw service in the Great War and afterwards export sales were built up. In 1928 the Indiana Company was acquired but after a few years it was sold off to the White Motor Company.

World War II saw production turned over to military contracts with a six-ton 6 × 6 chassis for carrying and unloading pontoon bridge parts. A similar chassis was produced for mounting heavy duty cranes, and as an aircraft crash tender.

Postwar production centred on the 260 series and then on further military vehicles for the Korean war.

A major step came in 1956 when Brockway became an autonomous division of Mack Trucks Inc, but the hand built system of production continued. 1958 saw the 'Huskie' range announced and the now familiar radiator mascot was introduced at the same time.

The first coe design appeared in 1963 and soon after the 300 series was introduced with 90 in. or 117 in. BBC dimensions. The shorter models are known as the 350 line and the longer as 360.

In Plate 1 is shown a stake bodied truck mounted on the Model 75 (JC type) chassis of 1928. This was of 7,500 lbs gross weight with a load capacity of 2,800 lbs. Wheelbase was 137 in. with a 96 in. body length. A six-cylinder, $3\frac{3}{8}$ in. bore × $4\frac{5}{8}$ in. stroke engine drove through a single dry plate clutch and four-speed gearbox to a spiral bevel rear axle. Mounted on 30 in. × 5 in. tyres the vehicle had a maximum speed of 45 mph.

NAG
[2]

During the trade depression years at the end of the 1920s many small manufacturers were forced to amalgamate or close down as the result of falling demand. This state of affairs existed on both sides of the Atlantic, and Germany was no exception.

Adam Opel was taken over by General Motors, Hansa Lloyd was acquired by Goliath, Elite Diamant shut up shop, and Mannesmann Mulag was absorbed by Bussing.

Bussing also took over NAG in 1931. The Nationale Automobil-Gesellschaft who had started in 1902 and during their lifetime had produced small vans, lorries, buses and agricultural tractors found themselves part of one of their competitors although they did manage to preserve their name in the title of the new set-up.

Soon after the take-over it was announced that Bussing NAG were going to use their added factory capacity to build $1\frac{1}{2}$- and 2-ton Adler-Bussings for the Adlerwerke of Frankfurt am Main.

In Plate 2 is shown a 1928 NAG street washer which could also be used for fire-fighting, a centrifugal pump being mounted for this purpose.

BIEDERMAN
[4]

Charles Biederman formed the company which bore his name in 1920 at Cincinnati, Ohio. He was determined that his trucks were going to be amongst the finest on the road so he gathered around himself a team of engineers, advertising each of them by name as responsible for the design and production of some particular part of the complete vehicle. He was particularly keen on the six-cylinder engine and managed to talk Continental into producing a narrow bore engine to his design. By March 1921 Biederman had the six-cylinder truck in their catalogue.

Other design features of which Biederman was proud were their patent variable rate rear springs which had a length of 65 in. for empty running and shortened to 43 in. when the vehicle was fully loaded. This was achieved by having the extreme ends of the springs bearing against hard cast steel wearing plates attached to the frame, and not bushed as is normal practice. In this design settlement of the springs under load caused them to flatten out against the wearing plates and so effectively shorten and stiffen the spring. Because the springs were unshackled, the rear axle was located by a pair of radius rods secured to the chassis frame by cast brackets.

Another feature of which they were very proud was the fact that even the $1\frac{1}{2}$-ton model had chassis frame rails 7 in. deep! Such was the strength and quality of the Biederman.

Plate 4 shows a 1928 Model 60 which was advertised as being a $2\frac{1}{2}$- to $3\frac{1}{2}$-ton model. This was the era of transition and it will be noted that the truck has 5 in. rubber cushion tyres at the front with 5 in. solid rubbers at the rear.

Other models of the period were the 20, a 1- to 1½-tonner and the 40 for 1½- to 2½-ton loads. All three models had the six-cylinder 3⅜ × 4½ in. 50 hp engine, multiplate clutch and progressive rear springs. Models 20 and 40 had three-speed gearboxes while the model 60 had a four-speed.

PAGEFIELD
[5]

The earliest vehicles for refuse collection were open horse-drawn carts into which the rubbish was tipped. Often these were not specially designed for the purpose and ladders had to be provided for the loaders. Later designs produced smaller wheels with a resulting lower load line. At first a plain sheet was used to cover the load on its trip to the tip, but later on attention was given to providing tailored canvas covers and then sheet metal covers which could be opened by hand or foot, being either sliding or hinged.

In small towns and parishes where the area of collection was small and the journey to the tip or incinerator short, the horse-drawn vehicle was adequate. As towns grew larger and expansion of housing estates pushed outward, the length of run from depot to collection area increased so horse teams spent more time in travelling and less in actual collection.

In order to overcome this state of affairs local councils turned to motor vehicles to speed up the turn-round of the collection teams, but some found that the cost of the equipment was excessive because of the constant running of the engine coupled with the frequent stops and starts associated with house-to-house collection.

The Pagefield system was one designed to get the best from both worlds – that of the horse for house-to-house collection and the motor vehicle for the longer non-stop journeys to the tip. Basically the system was to use a small wheeled horsedrawn refuse vehicle of either side or rear loading type which was fitted with quickly detachable shafts. When this trailer, cart or body was full the Pagefield motor vehicle would lower its ramps, the shafts would be detached, and the collection vehicle winched up onto the lorry (Plate 5). The Pagefield would be kept working by taking full carts to the tip and bringing them back empty to the same collection team or to another. In this way both the collectors and the journey vehicle were kept occupied in the task to which they were best suited.

CHEVROLET
[6]

'A Six for the Price of a Four' – thus ran one of the advertising slogans when the Chevrolet six-cylinder ohv engine was announced in 1928. The first truck model to have the new engine was the LQ of 1929.

The LQ was a $1\frac{1}{2}$-ton capacity truck of 10 ft 11 in. wheelbase. The six-cylinder petrol engine was of $3\frac{5}{16}$ in. bore $\times$ 4 in. stroke giving a displacement of 207 cu in. and was rated at 70 bhp at 3,200 rpm. Drive was by means of a single dry plate clutch through a four-speed gearbox and 4.9 : 1 ratio rear axle.

The chassis was 15 ft $7\frac{1}{2}$ in. overall and was carried on steel disc wheels shod with 30 in. $\times$ 5 in. front tyres and 32 in. $\times$ 6 in. single rear tyres.

In Britain the Chevrolet $1\frac{1}{2}$-tonner was the forerunner of the Bedford 2-tonner which made its appearance in 1931. General Motors truck plant was at Hendon originally but after the acquisition of Vauxhall in 1925 GM had the facilities at Luton to start a better truck production line. The first Bedford models were the 2-ton WHG and WLG which were powered by the Chevrolet design six-cylinder engine and the WHG was of the same wheelbase as the old LQ model.

Plate 6 shows an LQ model of 1929 which is one produced in Belgium. During the 1920s General Motors – of which Chevrolet had been a part since 1918 – opened plants at Hendon, Copenhagen and Antwerp for the assembly of trucks shipped in CKD form from America and Canada.

BERNA
[7]

Established in 1904 at Olten in Switzerland, Berna soon gained a reputation for producing quality vehicles capable of heavy work. Within a few years a vigorous export business was promoted with sales being recorded in Britain, Australia, Italy, Canada, Ireland and Austria.

The early vehicles employed shaft drive to a bevel rear axle and thence by axle shafts to internal ring gear on the rear wheels. The weight of the rear axle was taken by a massive, curved box section dead axle and the torque reaction was absorbed by a pair of long radius rods which terminated in brackets bolted under the chassis beneath the driver's seat. From the mid 1920s this drive system was replaced by the more orthodox Hotchkiss system with a live axle driving through the wheel centre and the torque reaction taken by the road springs.

Plate 7 shows a Berna which was operating in Britain from the late 1920s. This model and its predecessors were quite popular on the British market and for some years around World War I, a works was established in Kensington, London for assembly of the Berna under the title of British Berna.

The vehicle shown was in service until 1952, being used for the transport of frozen carcasses of meat from the London Docks to Smithfield and other meat markets. The heavy wooden body is in fact a lift van or container specially constructed for meat transport. The whole body is of double skinned construction using tongued and grooved boards with four inches of cork insulation between them for temperature control.

MORRIS COMMERCIAL
[8]

The first Morris Commercial appeared in 1924. It was the Model T, a four cylinder (75 mm × 102 mm) 28 bhp engined 20-cwt

19

truck with 10 ft 2 in. wheelbase and 13 ft 6 in. overall length. A three-speed gearbox and a worm driven rear axle were fitted and the vehicle was carried on 32 in. × 4½ in. tyres.

In 1925 a 12-cwt model was added, and in 1927 there were seven models including a six-wheeler and one on Roadless tracks. By 1932 the range was up to 15 trucks and seven passenger chassis, and during the 1930s production was concentrated on models in the 15-cwt to 5-ton payload class.

Plate 8 shows a van mounted on the 'Dictator' chassis which was first introduced at the 1929 Olympia Show. The model was of 25 ft 4 in. overall length with a wheelbase of 16 ft 4½ in. Power was produced by a new Morris Commercial six-cylinder petrol engine of 110 bhp (at 2,600 rpm) from a capacity of 7013 cc. A single dry plate clutch and four-speed gearbox were fitted and the rear axle was of the underslung worm type with fully floating axle shafts.

Actual deliveries of the chassis did not commence until the end of 1930 because a new factory at Adderley Park had to be completed before the 'Dictator' and other heavy chassis in the range could be produced. The old Soho factory was being used for the production of the lighter vehicles in the range.

From 1932 a longer wheelbase version of the 'Dictator' was available (18 ft 0 in.), and from 1933 a larger engine of 110 mm × 135 mm was used. This continued until the model was dropped from the range in 1936 when the company decided to concentrate their efforts on goods vehicles in the medium capacity range and discontinued making passenger models, of which the 'Dictator' was one.

FWD ENGLAND
[9]

In Plate 9 is shown a particular type of half track produced by FWD England for the Royal National Lifeboat Institution and used in connection with the launching and recovery of lifeboats which were carried on a special tracked trailer.

These special FWDs were a derivation of the FWD/AEC 6 × 6

model R6T tractor which was produced by Four Wheel Drive Motors Ltd of Slough using AEC components, and later became known as FWD England.

In Britain the FWD had its origins during World War I when many of the original model B army 4 × 4 3-tonners saw service with the British armed forces in Europe. During the 1920s civilian production included a low loading dustcart using the FWD front wheel drive unit while the rear end was mounted on small solid rubber tyred wheels. This type was also offered as a load carrier. Another unorthodox design was for a small wheeled three-wheeler which was not a success.

In the late 1920s a long wheelbase six-wheeler was designed which had considerable cross country capabilities even whilst towing a trailer. In 1929 the prototype R6T tractor was produced and a number of these saw service with the British army as gun tractors and as recovery vehicles.

The R6T was powered by an AEC six-cylinder petrol engine (100 mm × 130 mm) which produced 96 bhp at 2,500 rpm. Drive was through a single dry plate clutch and four-speed gearbox to a transfer box where the drive was divided to the front and rear axles.

KARRIER
[10]

For very many years the railway cartage experts in Britian had been studying the waste of having power units standing idle while the load-carrying part of their vehicles, both horse and motor, was being loaded.

During the 1920s it was becoming obvious that the days of horse transport were rapidly coming to a close and an additional factor was that the horse-drawn carts could be given a further lease of life by being adapted for use with motors.

Various ideas were tried including quickly detachable horse shafts, horse carts with detachable front axles, demountable bodies and various types of articulated vehicles.

At the instigation of the London, Midland and Scottish Railway Company, Karrier Motors of Huddersfield produced a prototype light tractor unit which was the progenitor of a long line of tractor/trailer outfits used by this and other railways over the years to come (Plate 10).

The original design, called the 'Cob' and introduced in 1931, was actually of two types. One type had hydraulically actuated jaws at the rear of the chassis which lifted the axle of the horse cart bodily onto the tractor chassis frame, while the other had an inclined ramp at the rear which could be backed under a suitably modified horse vehicle which had a pair of hinged legs fitted in place of the forecarriage.

Within a short while of the LMSR prototypes entering service the three other mainline railway companies ordered 'Cobs' for their delivery services. One design was for the horsecart forecarriage to be replaced by a pair of small diameter wheels mounted on a turntable. These wheels were of a wider track than the rear wheels of the tractor unit so that when coupled the cart wheels were raised clear of the ground and positioned outside those of the tractor.

Briefly, the Karrier 'Cob' was a three wheeled tractor unit of 8 ft 8 in. wheelbase with a 3 ft 5½ in. rear track. It had an overall chassis length of 11 ft 9 in. and was capable of turning within a 16 ft diameter circle. At the rear end the ground clearance was a mere four inches!

The chassis was powered by the well known Jowett 7 hp horizontally opposed twin engine of 907 cc rated at 17 bhp, driving through a single dry plate clutch and three-speed gearbox to a bevel rear axle. Tyre size was 18 in. × 5 in. (solid rubbers) but 22 in. × 5 in. were available if required. At an engine speed of 2,000 rpm the road speed was just over 12 mph.

The Karrier three-wheeler was also available as a load carrying chassis and this model was designated the 'Colt'. With a generally similar specification to the 'Cob' the 'Colt' differed by way of having an overall chassis length of 13 ft 10 in. and track of 4 ft 8 in. Rated load capacity was 2 tons as against 3 for the articulated 'Cob'.

MERCEDES BENZ
[11]

During the early 1920s Benz, Saurer and MAN were all working on their designs for small, high speed oil engines for road vehicle use. In 1923 the Benz was ready for use and was duly installed in a 5-ton chassis. This was the four-cylinder engine of 125 mm bore and 180 mm stroke.

In Britain the Benz engine was taken up by McLaren who built the engines under licence and one of these was fitted in the Kerr Stuart lorry first introduced in 1929.

Just prior to this, in April 1928 the first Mercedes Benz diesel engined vehicles were imported into Britain, two 5/6-ton models powered by a six-cylinder engine of 105 mm bore and 165 mm stroke. These were L5 types numbered MU 61073 and MU 61078 and it was by RAC tests of these vehicles in September 1928 that Mercedes Benz gained the Dewar Trophy for fuel economy.

Plate 11 shows an NK56 model rigid six-wheeler for 10-ton loads. This machine had a wheelbase of 19 ft 2 in. and was carried on 13.5 in. section tyres mounted all round on Simplex cast spoke wheels. The six-cylinder (105 mm × 165 mm) engine was fitted and drive was by means of a single plate clutch and eight-speed gearbox.

LEYLAND
[12]

Toward the end of 1931 Leylands introduced two additional models to their popular range of goods vehicles, the four wheeled 'Buffalo' and six wheeled 'Rhino'. The models were of similar basic layout, being of normal control but with a set back front axle giving, in the words of the brochure, 'maximum engine accessibility, a full width cab and correct distribution of the load.'

The Buffalo was rated as $7\frac{1}{4}$ ton and the Rhino as $12\frac{1}{2}$ ton gross load capacity chassis, this being the first time that this manufacturer had stated vehicle capacity in such a manner. This was because some operators were buying a '5 tonner', adding a very heavy body and then expecting the vehicle to carry maximum loads, which was tantamount to using the vehicle beyond the safe limit envisaged by the manufacturer.

Illustrated in Plate 12 is the 'Rhino' which was delivered to Hovis Ltd, the flour millers, after appearing at the 1931 Olympia Show. In its original guise a heavy boarded tilt body was fitted to the chassis. After a while this was replaced by a metal bulk hopper type body which had provision for loading through the roof at dockside silos and discharging of the load through floor hatches at the delivery point. Double doors were fitted at the rear so that bagged grain could be carried as required.

The original engine specified for the Rhino was a Leyland six-cylinder petrol engine of $4\frac{9}{16}$ in. bore and $5\frac{1}{2}$ in. stroke, but the then new Leyland 8 litre oil engine was also available as an alternative ($4\frac{3}{8}$ in. $\times$ $5\frac{1}{2}$ in.). Drive was by means of a single dry plate clutch to a four-speed gearbox and thence by two-speed auxiliary gearbox to a double reduction single drive rear bogie. For most of its length the chassis frame was 12 in. deep with a steel flitch plate for the rearmost 18 feet in order to provide ample strength in the load bearing area.

CARDEN-LOYD
[13]

In Plate 13 is shown one of the few fully tracked vehicles produced for civilian purposes – the Carden-Loyd Tractor Truck produced by Vickers-Armstrong Ltd, in 1931.

This company had gained considerable experience of tracked vehicles because of military contracts for trucks and armoured cars, and thought that there was demand for a tracked vehicle in underdeveloped regions of the world.

The Carden-Loyd was designed to carry a load of $1\frac{1}{2}$ tons and tow a trailer of up to 6 tons in weight. Power was supplied by a six-cylinder petrol engine driving through a five-speed gearbox and thence by way of cross shafts incorporating multiple plate clutches for steering, to the drive sprockets at the front.

Unladen weight of the tractor truck was $2\frac{3}{4}$ tons; it measured 12 ft in length, 6 ft 2 in. in width and 6 ft 2 in. overall height. The body was 6 ft 4 in. long and 5 ft 11 in. wide inside.

BEARDMORE
[14]

In Plate 14 is shown a Beardmore tractor in the fleet of Watney, Combe Reid and Company, the brewers of Mortlake, Surrey. Watneys had a handful of these tractors during the 1930s for towing drawbar trailers between the brewery and the bottling stores. The trailers were stainless steel beer tanks clad with wood to give the appearance of an enormous beer barrel.

When the drawbar trailers were ousted in favour of articulated trailers drawn by Scammell 'Mechanical Horse' and Dennis 'Horla' type tractors the trailer tanks had the locking forecarriage removed and Scammell automatic coupling gear substituted for a further lease of life.

The Beardmore tractors were relegated to shunting duties for the few drawbar trailers retained for certain trunk vehicles and the one depicted in our plate occasionally took a load of beer for export to the docks. A similar tractor located at the Yarmouth Maltings was fitted with buffing equipment for handling bulk malt railway wagons.

Beardmore tractors were of the French Chenard-Walcker design and were publicised in Britain by a 10,000 mile non-stop journey in 1931. In due course the Beardmore was produced entirely in Britain except for the Chenard Walcker patent towing device which enabled a variable amount of the trailer weight to be superimposed on the driving axle of the tractor in order to increase adhesion as required.

The vehicles became known as Beardmore Multiwheelers with a factory at Clapham and from 1932 as Multiwheelers with a plant under the railway line at Harrow. In 1934 the firm became Multiwheelers (Commerical Vehicles) Ltd and production of the Cobra Python and Anaconda types continued, but toward the end of the 1930s production appeared to cease although trailers were produced until some time later.

AEC
[15 and 16]

The vehicle depicted in Plates 15 and 16 is a special type of AEC tractor, towing two eight-wheeled trailers for operation across unmade country. Several of these outfits were built in the 1930s for operation in the Gold Coast, Russia and Australia, and at least one is still surviving in the last mentioned country.

It was in 1927 that the British Colonial Office Conference discussed the problems associated with transport in underdeveloped countries with little or no railway or road system. The conference thought that it would be better to operate road trains than to go to the high first cost of providing railway facilities, but there were many problems of detail to be overcome before the scheme could be implemented. In order to draw up the requirements in a practical way the Overseas Mechanical Directing Committee was set up to make recommendations.

The outcome of these deliberations was an eight-wheeled tractor towing eight-wheeled trailers designed to transport a 15-ton payload over unmade roads. The first tractor was a petrol-engined vehicle built by Leyland Motors and it was shipped to the Gold Coast for feasibility trails.

From the results obtained with this first tractor which worked the 240 miles between Kamusi and Tamale, it was decided to build a similar outfit but with a compression-ignition engine.

This time it was AEC who built the vehicle and the first of these was completed in 1933. As mentioned above the road train consisted of the tractor unit and two trailers, with identical running units but with differing body designs. Each unit was mounted on two four-wheel bogies fitted with 10.5 in. $\times$ 20 in. tyres inflated to 38 lbs per sq in. which were sufficient to carry the vehicle and its load over dry river beds or soil roads without fear of bogging down.

The tractor unit was powered by the AEC 130 hp six-cylinder CI engine, which drove all four axles via four-speed gearbox mounted behind the engine and a three-speed gearbox fitted further down the chassis. Drive to the axles was via a set of three gears at the extreme end of the drive shaft and then to the four worm-driven axles. The first and fourth axles steered and the two inner axles were Westinghouse-braked.

Trailers for the road train were the product of R A Dyson and Company Limited of Liverpool and consisted of bodies mounted on two four-wheel bogies with sliding turntables. The bogies were connected in order to make the trailers track behind the tractor.

BERLIET
[17]

Camions Berliet date from the turn of the century, and since the 1920s this marque has produced the majority of vehicles for the French heavy vehicle market. Berliet took up the idea of gas producers and diesel engines very early in the development periods of these forms of power, and have produced diesel engines for buses, boats, railway carriages, shunting locomotives, generating sets and of course trucks.

As early as 1931 Berliet had nine types of diesel engine catalogued, of both four- and six-cylinder layout. In the four-cylinder range were engines of 100 mm × 140 mm, 110 mm × 150 mm and 120 mm × 160 mm sizes, while the six-cylinder engines were made in 110 mm × 150 mm, 120 mm × 160 mm, 130 mm × 160 mm, 130 mm × 180 mm and 135 mm × 180 mm dimensions.

In an effort to get transport operators to better understand the savings possible by the use of diesel engines, Berliet arranged a run by two vehicles over a route between Lille and Marseille. One vehicle was powered by the orthodox petrol engine while the second was diesel engined. The petrol engine installed was a six-cylinder 8 litre unit, while the diesel was a 10.8 litre six-cylinder engine of 120 mm × 160 mm size. Both vehicles were loaded with 7,500 kg and run over the 1,100-kilometre route while the fuel consumption was carefully monitored.

The petrol engine consumed 715 litres of fuel at a cost of Fr 1,251 while the diesel used only 385 litres at a cost of Fr 385.

The Berliet lorry shown in Plate 17 is a long wheelbase six-wheeler of 15 tons capacity with a double deck livestock body. This model is powered by the six-cylinder 10.8 litre engine.

SHELVOKE AND DREWRY
[18]

The Shelvoke and Drewry 'Freighter Dust Cart' was designed primarily as a municipal vehicle and was not an adaptation of an everyday commercial vehicle. Its attributes were a low loading line, ability to travel very slowly, good load distribution and ability to be driven by someone unskilled.

The first design appeared in 1923 and the now familiar sheet front panel, small diameter wheels and two handle control made it easily recognisable during the next forty years or so. In later years the design was modified to keep up with changing demands in the municipal vehicle market, and the tiller steering was replaced by the accepted steering wheel. A completely enclosed cab was fitted before the war and tyre sizes increased for greater carrying capacity. The old canvas or sheet metal dust covers have given way to more sophisticated designs of barrier, moving floor, tipping and compression type refuse bodies. One quite rare type produced has been a six-wheel street washer for the City of Westminster.

Although originally designed as a municipal vehicle, S and D chassis have been used for such other applications as tankers, mobile shops, laundry vans (see Volume 1 Plate 122), glass carriers, milk delivery trucks, works trucks and seafront buses.

A normal type of chassis with axles suspended on semi-elliptic springs was used but the four-cylinder engine was mounted across the frame at the front right hand side. The driver sat in the centre with controls consisting of one lever for steering at his right, and another for gear changing at his left.

The provision of mechanically operated signal arms for following traffic was a feature of S and D vehicles because of the centre control.

The SD was a unique style of vehicle and enjoyed great popularity among municipal users. Many other vehicles builders such as Garner, Vulcan, Lowdeck, Guy, Carrimore and Easyloader produced models aimed at the same market but none gained the same share as that by Shelvoke and Drewry.

Plate 18 shows a typical refuse vehicle of the 1930s, a 10 cubic yard capacity Chelsea type with sliding covers to contain the refuse and double hinged doors at the rear which are opened when the load is tipped at the site or into barges.

DODGE
[19]

The Dodge name goes back to the year 1914 when the first vehicle to bear the name of the Dodge Brothers was built, a private car. A short while after the first business car or commercial screen sided truck was produced. As from 1925 the trucks became known as Graham Brothers after an agreement was made with this old Dodge bodybuilding firm. In 1928 control of Dodge and Graham Brothers passed to the Chrysler Corporation.

Illustrated in Plate 19 is a model from the 1935 range of Dodge trucks – the model KC sedan van on the 111 in. wheelbase chassis. The KC model was available in chassis/scuttle, pickup, sedan van, panel van or open van with side screen forms. A slightly longer wheelbase of 119 in. was offered (model KCL) as an alternative. The engine was a six-cylinder petrol unit of $3\frac{1}{8}$ in. bore and $4\frac{3}{8}$ in. stroke and rated at 70 bhp. Of about $\frac{1}{2}$-ton capacity, the model was replaced by the MC in 1937.

The present range of Dodge trucks runs from the D100/200/300 pick-up models and the W100/200/300 power wagons through the B100/200/300 Tradesman, KaryVan and Maxivans, the medium duty D500/600/800 and W600 trucks, the heavy duty short conventional CN800 and CNT800 trucks, the heavy duty LCF diesel trucks and tilt trucks LS1000 and LT 1000 to the latest 'Bighorn' models CN950 and CNT950.

The payload spread is from an unspecified amount on the smallest pick-up through to 76,800 pounds gross combined weight for the LT1000 6 × 4 tractor.

Engines available include a slant six-cylinder and V8 petrol for the pick-ups and vans, V8 .petrol engines for the medium duty models, V8 petrol or Cummins and Caterpillar diesels in the truck range and Cummins or Detroit Diesels in the heaviest models.

MERAY
[20]

Plate 20 shows an unusual vehicle produced in Hungary during 1935. This is a 1-ton capacity light truck produced by a firm called Meray, who named this model the Tehertaxi which means goods or load taxi, and it certainly boasted some novel features.

The chassis frame was made of welded steel tube with additional strengthening by steel angle trussing below the outer sides of the wooden drop side body.

Power was supplied by a three-cylinder four-stroke radial petrol engine of some 22 hp. This power unit was mounted at the rear of the vehicle and was in unit with a four-speed gearbox and the rear axle.

The absence of any mechanical drive units at the front part of the vehicle made it possible for the cab to be positioned at a low level, thus giving easy access by just one step.

THE COLOUR PLATES

1   1928   Brockway stake body truck   USA

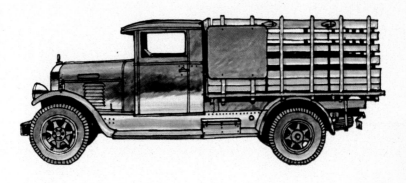

2   1928   NAG street washer   Germany

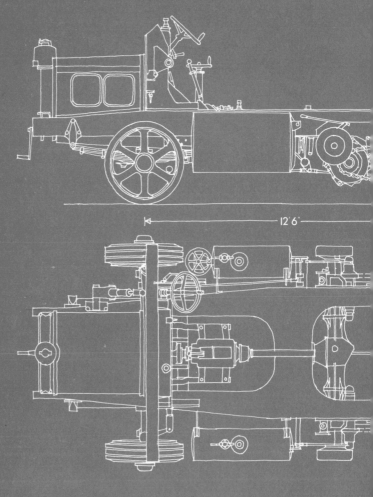

12'6"

3   1929   Scammell 100-ton tractor unit   Britain

| 0 | 1 | 2 | 3 | 4 | 5 | 6ft |

4   1928   Biederman removals truck   USA

5   1928   Pagefield refuse container lorry   Britain

6 1929 Chevrolet 1½-ton LQ model USA/Belgium

7 1929 Berna insulated meat van Switzerland

8   1930   Morris Commercial 'Dictator' van   Britain

9   1929   FWD halftrack lifeboat tractor   Britain

10   1931   Karrier 'Cob' motor horse   Britain

11   1931   Mercedes Benz 10-ton six-wheeler   Germany

12   1931   Leyland 'Rhino' van   Britain

13   1931   Carden-Loyd tractor truck   Britain

14   1932   Beardmore brewery tractor   Britain

15 1933 AEC road train Britain

16 1933 AEC overseas tractor Britain

De Transport Rapides De Bestiaux PARIS

17   1934   Berliet double-deck livestock truck   France

18   1935   Shelvoke & Drewry freighter   Britain

19   1935   Dodge model KC sedan van   USA

20   1935   Meray rear-engined truck   Hungary

21   1936   MAN 4 ton-van and trailer   Germany

22   1936   Scammell oilfield tanker   Britain

23   1936   Ford 'Tug' tractor and trailer   Britain

24   1936   Electricar-Scammell refuse collector   Britain

25   1937   Wilson electric advertising van   Britain

26   1937   Dodge Travellers Brougham   Britain

27   1936   Clydesdale 1½-ton van   USA

28   1937   Latil and roadrail tank   France/Britain

29   1936   Union and insulated meat trailers   Britain

30   1939   Renault 10-ton six-wheeler   France

31   1939   Tatra showing backbone chassis   Czechoslovakia

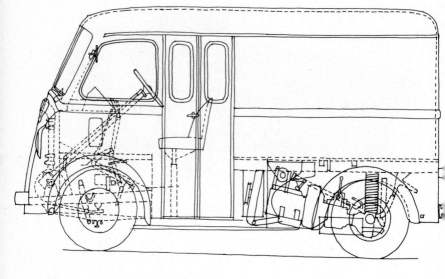

32　　1939　White Horse delivery van　　USA

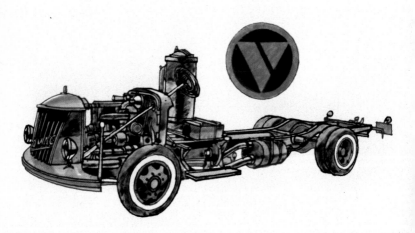

33　　1940　Vomag chassis with gas producer　　Germany

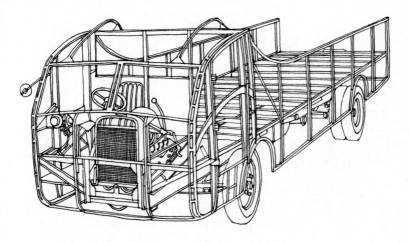

34   1939   JNSN lightweight lorry   Britain

35   1940   Albion CX27 twin-steer lorry   Britain

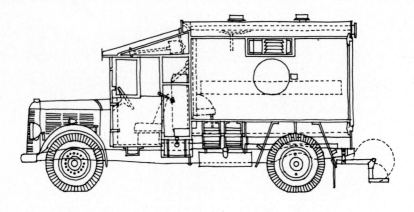

36   1940   Bedford ML military ambulance   Britain

37   1938   Scammell 'Pioneer' oilfield tractor   Britain

38   1938   Scammell 'Mechanical Horse' tractor   Britain

39   1940   Scammell 'Showboat' parcels van   Britain

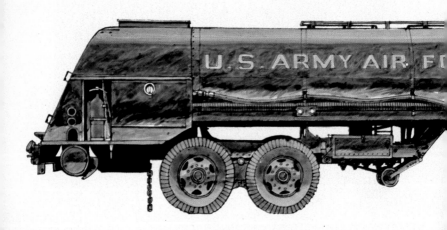

40   1943   Reo aviation fuel tanker   USA

41   1944   Diamond T heavy haulage tractor   USA

42   1946   Scammell ballasted tractor   Britain

43　1944　Bedford 'QL' forestry tractor　Britain

45   1948   Scammell frameless tanker   Britain

46   1947   FIAT lorry and trailer   Italy

47 1947 Proctor Mark I 6-tonner Britain

48   1940s   Mack LM six-wheeler   USA

49   1949   GMC double-bottom tank rig   USA

50 1950 Maudslay 'Meritor' eight-wheeler Britain

51 1950 .Brown tandem tractor USA

52   1948   Austin '3-way' delivery van   Britain

53   1951   Jowett 'Bradford' 5-cwt van   Britain

54   1955   Guy 'Goliath' eight-wheeler   Britain

55   1954   AEC 'Mammoth Major Mark III' tanker   Britain

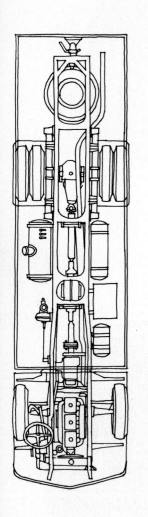

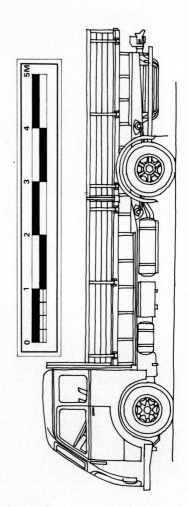

56   1954   FBW L40v 6-ton truck   Switzerland

0   1   2   3   4   5M

57   1953   Commer 'QX' underfloor engined tractor   Britain

58   1954   Bristol 'HG' eight-wheeler and trailer   Britain

60 1954 Coleman-Marmon-Herrington snowplough USA

61   1961   Alfa Romeo 'Mille'   Italy

62   1961   Douglas 'Tugmaster' shunter   Britain

63   1957   Rutland 'Stuka' twin-steer   Britain

64   1961   Norde high-speed tractor   Britain

65   1962   TVW eight-wheel tipper   Britain

66   1958   Dennis 'Paravan' parcels van   Britain

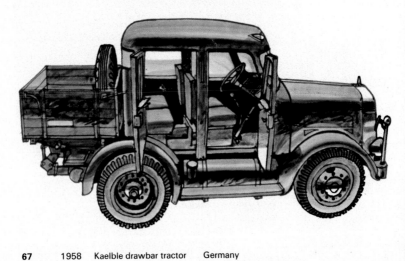

67   1958   Kaelble drawbar tractor   Germany

68   1968   Praga 6×6 tanker   Czechoslovakia

69   1965   Hendrickson tridem tipper   USA

70   1962   W & E articulated milk float   Britain

71   1956   Divco delivery van   USA

72 1965 Nazar tipper Spain

73 1964 Steagul Rosu 'Carpati' 3-ton truck Rumania

74   1965   Hanomag low-loading delivery truck   Germany

75   1962   White aircraft refueller   USA

76   1963   Mowag with front door cab   Switzerland

77   1963   Mowag steel carrier with trailer   Switzerland

78 1963 FAR 'Mechanical Horse' France

79 1963 Willeme LF model tractor France

80   1965   Oshkosh 8×8 tractor   USA

81   1966   Bussing 'Decklaster' pallet vehicle   Germany

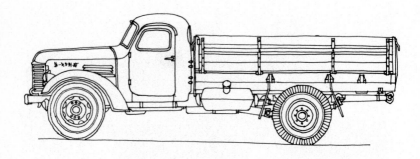

82   1965   Jay-Fong 4-ton truck   China

83   1966   Atkinson bulk salt carrier   Britain

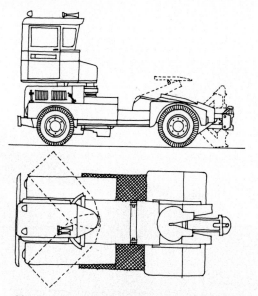

84a 1967 FMC Terminal Tug yard hustler USA

84b 1967 FMC Terminal Tug with swivel cab USA

85   1966   Sisu heavy haulage tractor   Finland

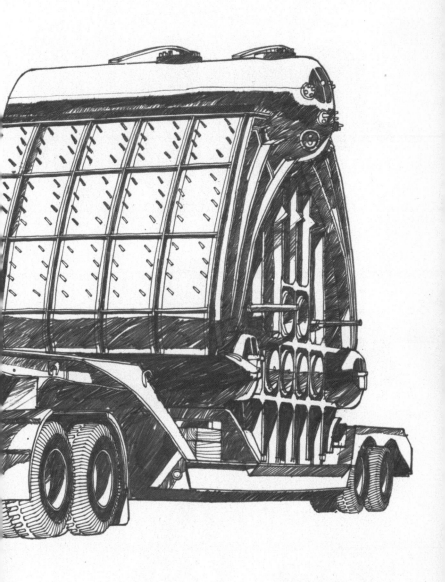

87   1968   Star 6×6 truck   Poland

88   1967   Cline heavy duty tractor   USA

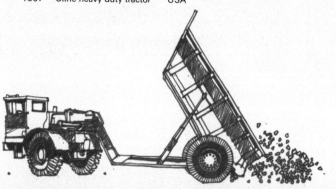

89   c1970   Isco articulated rear dump   USA

90   c1970   Isco 60-ton molten slag hauler   USA

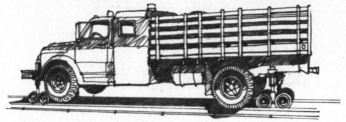

91   c1970   Isco railroad conversion for trucks   USA

92   c1970   Isco yard shunter coupled to road trailer   USA

93   c1970   Isco yard shunter moving boxcars.   USA

94   c1969   Sicard 'Snowmaster' at work   Canada

95   c1970   Walter wingplow snowfighter   USA

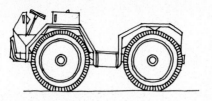

96   c1970   Walter aircraft tractor   USA

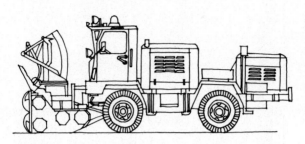

97   c1970   Walter snowfighter   USA

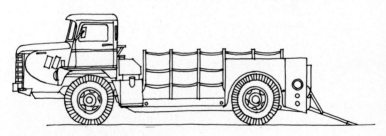

98   c1970   Walter front-drive low bed truck   USA

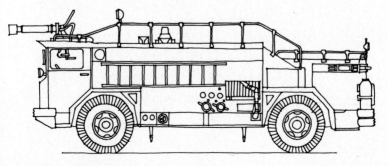

99   c1970   Walter aircraft crash tender   USA

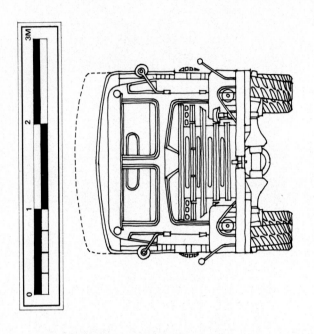

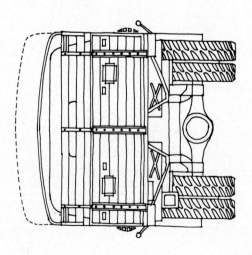

3M
0   1   2

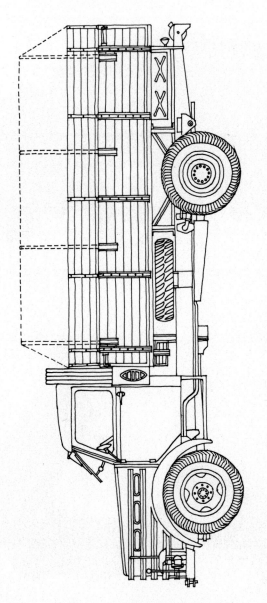

100   1963   Csepel 'D344' 4×4 truck   Hungary

101   1970   Zil 131 6×6 cargo truck   USSR

102   1970   Kraz 256b 12,000kg tipper   USSR

103   1970   Zil 130 6,000kg truck   USSR

104   1961   Zil 157K 6×6 snowplough   USSR

105   1970   Kraz 255b 6×6 cross country truck   USSR

106   1970   Gaz 66 4×4 cross country truck   USSR

107 1970 Ural 375D 6×6 cross country truck USSR

108 1973 Kamaz prototype drawbar outfit USSR

109   1973   Kamaz prototype tipper   USSR

110   1972   Mol 6×6 tipper   Belgium

111   1967   Kalmar Swedish post van   Sweden

112   1967   Holden 'Belmont' panel van   Australia

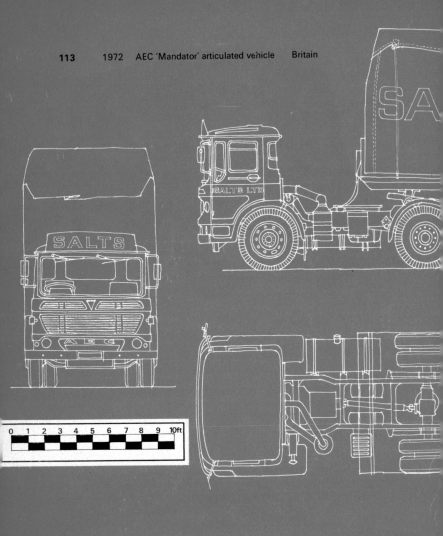

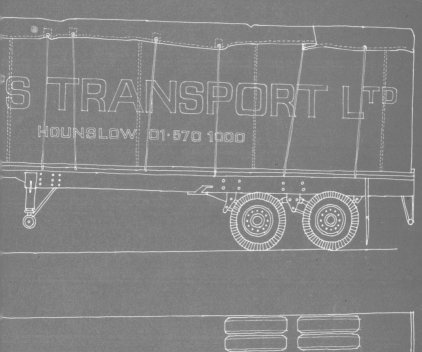

114 1971 FAUN heavy haulage tractor Germany

115 1972 Autocar articulated dump USA

116   1970   Ralph heavy duty tractor   South Africa

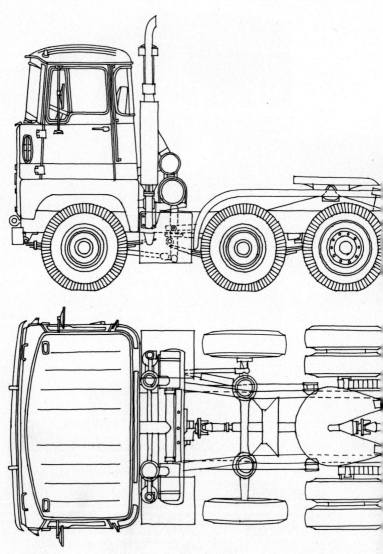

117   1970   Scammell 'Samson' 75-ton tractor   Britain

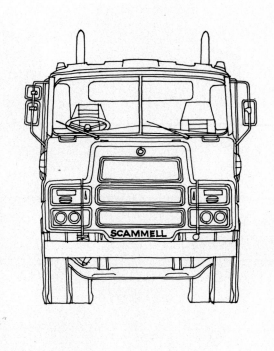

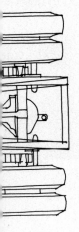

0 1 2 3 4 5 6ft

118   1971   Henschel double-drive tractor   Germany

120   1972   Peterbilt bottom dump   USA

121   1972   Volvo aircraft refueller   Sweden

122   1973   International 17,000 gallon tanker   USA

MAN
[21]

The MAN concern gets its title from Machinenfabrik Augsburg Nurnburg and began vehicle production by producing Swiss Saurers under licence.

Because of the close connection between the celebrated German engineer Dr Rudolf Diesel and the MAN company it was only natural that an early entry into the compression ignition engine market should be made by them.

There is still some argument as to who built the first auomotive diesel engine because many designs were made and some models were actually displayed quite early in the century, but Benz and MAN were just about neck and neck during the early 1920s. A MAN lorry was shown at the 1924 Berlin Motor Show complete with a four-cylinder diesel engine and several of this type were subsequently bought by the Bavarian Post Office.

By 1932 MAN were producing only diesel engines, so confident were they that the future for the heavy lorry lay in the use of the oil engine.

A model from the 1936 range is shown in Plate 21. This is a D1 4-ton chassis powered by the type DO540 six-cylinder diesel engine which produced 90 bhp at 1,800 rpm from its 105 mm bore × 140 mm stroke cylinders.

FORD
[23]

One of the most unusual Ford trucks to be marketed in Britain must surely be the 'Tug' which was publicly announced in October 1935 (Plate 23).

The 'Tug' was a three wheeled tractor unit which embodied much of the current model Y, designated for small cars and 5-cwt vans. It was produced with a trailer coupling pin bolted to the rear chassis cross-member but a caravan type of coupling with a 2 in. ball could be substituted and some other dealers fitted a special ramped plate for the automatic pick-up of trailers suitably constructed.

The tractor was designed to tow either two- or four-wheel trailers or those partially superimposed by the automatic type coupling. Whatever type of trailer was adopted the load was quoted as 2 tons.

In the mid 1930s there was a lot of activity with the mechanical horse type of tractor and no doubt Ford had this in mind when the 'Tug' was designed. However it did not sell in very great numbers and was not available after 1937. At least one company marketed the 'Tug' as a rigid three-wheel van but with a longer wheelbase than standard.

Brief Specification
   Wheelbase: 88½ in.
   Overall length: 120 in.
   Overall width: 69 in.
   Overall height: 66¾ in.
   Turning circle (tractor): 16 ft
   Front suspension by coil spring
   Rear suspension by transverse springs
   Four-cylinder petrol engine of 933 cc producing 22 bhp
      at 3,500 rpm
   Dry single plate clutch
   Four speed gearbox
   Spiral bevel rear axle located by radius rods

ELECTRICAR SCAMMELL
[24]

'A quart in a pint pot' – that was the advertising slogan of the Eagle Compressmore refuse collector which found many users during the 1930s.

Although not to the same extent as today, household refuse

114

collection during the years leading up to World War II was nevertheless a battle against the ever increasing amount of packaging which was being produced by industry in order to convey, protect and proclaim its products. Local councils were finding that collection costs were rising as the bulk increased and the natural reaction was to look for some means of compressing the refuse in the collection vehicle because although it had great bulk it was not necessarily dense.

Many designs of vehicle graced the streets of our towns and cities. There were those which tipped in order to get the refuse up to the front of the van, there were some which had a moving floor to move the refuse forwards, there was another type which rotated to ensure that the body was filled, and then there was the 'Eagle Compressmore' which did just that.

The articulated refuse vehicles of the City of Westminster (Plate 24) were almost unique. They were quite large as refuse vehicles go (approximately 20 cu. yds) and were propelled by an unusual three-wheeled tractor unit which embodied running units by Scammell Lorries and electrical equipment by Electricar. The articulated battery electric design was chosen for several reasons. In the City of Westminster a large part of the refuse collection service has to be carried out at night owing to the pure volume of traffic using the crowded streets. The near-silence of the electric vehicle is therefore an advantage. The articulated layout was useful in that different trailers could be handled and it gave room for a more capacious body with low loading height.

The Electricar TV6 tractor was a 10 ft 1 in. wheelbase machine with 29 in. × 8 in. front tyre and 10.5 in. × 13 in. twin rears. Power was produced by a 44 cell battery by Young Accumulator of 364 amps capacity and was mounted in panniers on either side of the chassis frame. The chassis, axles and suspension were as in the Scammell 6-ton mechanical horse.

In addition to refuse collection work these tractors were also used for towing Dennis gulley emptiers and street washers, and moving floor type refuse trailers.

When these interesting articulated electrics came up for renewal in 1960 Westminster City Council still felt that the idea of electrics was still valid and both Dennis Brothers and Seddon Diesel Vehicles produced for consideration prototype tractor chassis suitably adapted for battery electric propulsion.

WILSON ELECTRIC

For very many years the local carnival, fête or fair has been used by tradesmen as a showplace for their wares. Wherever there are people it is only natural that publicity minded producers will do all they can to show what they have to offer.

Years ago it was the horsedrawn turnout which was used as a base for the publicity vehicle and with the advent of the motor van it was quickly realised that there was a highly mobile and more compact outfit to be used.

So the sphere of the advertising vehicle took on a new lease of life and novel designs appeared thick and fast. Within a short space of time we were treated to the sight of mobile toothpaste tubes, tea boxes, biscuit tins, vacuum cleaners, houses, refrigerators, beer barrels, fountain pens, cookers, tyres, beer bottles and even a bath!

In some instances the vehicles were used solely for advertising purposes and spent their lives touring carnivals, fairs, fêtes, seaside resorts, shop openings and anything else which attracted people. Other vehicles did actually perform a transport function and it is to the credit of some motor bodybuilders that they achieved carrying capacity within some of the designs.

The vehicle shown in Plate 25 is a Wilson electric van chassis with an electric cooker design of the 1930s used by an electrical undertaking. This was in the days when certain industries tried to be true to their calling and we saw gas company vehicles running on coke and electric power supply companies using battery electrics.

DODGE
[26]

Established in Britain in 1923, Dodge trucks were built in Fulham and Willesden before production was started at Kew in 1928 following the acquisition of Dodge by Chrysler.

The Kew-built Dodge was for many years a hybrid of British and American units but by 1938 it was produced entirely in Britain.

One of the Kew productions of the pre-war era is shown in Plate 26. This is what was termed the Commercial Traveller's Brougham or Gown Van and is a vehicle specially designed for the carriage of hanging garments. The transport of clothing calls for special vehicles because the garments are best carried hanging from the roof. By this method the van can be completedly filled with goods with little risk of damage or creasing. Because the weight is carried by the roof rails the method of construction is important, and for stability when cornering rails or panels are provided low down inside the body to prevent the load from swinging.

The van illustrated is mounted on a Dodge MCX 15-cwt chassis with 116 in. wheelbase. A six-cylinder $2\frac{7}{8}$ in. $\times$ $4\frac{1}{8}$ in. engine of 70 bhp is fitted and drive is through a three-speed gearbox to a spiral bevel rear axle.

CLYDESDALE
[27]

Although truck production started in 1928 and is believed to have ceased in 1937, a small range of Clydesdale trucks were listed for another couple of years. Production was mostly in the medium weight range and being one of the smaller producers the company found the going very difficult during the early 1930s.

In an effort to stay in business and yet not have too much competition a switch to diesel engined trucks was made in 1934. The small range was first offered about the middle of 1935 and consisted of the 34D model for $1\frac{1}{2}$-ton load, 44D for 2 tons, 54D for $2\frac{1}{2}$ tons, 90D for 4 tons and the 7-ton capacity 105D. These vehicles were fitted with Buda or Hercules engines, the 34D being a four-cylinder while the others were of six-cylinder configuration.

By 1937 the range had increased to eleven models covering a payload range of $1\frac{1}{2}$ to 10 tons, or almost a different model listing for each additional ton carried! Again power was supplied by

117

Buda or Hercules diesel engines, nine of the eleven models being six-cylinder type.

In 1938 the range offered had been reduced to eight models in the 2-ton to 15-ton load classes. Only the smallest (34D) was a four-cylinder type, and by this time only Buda engines were listed.

A similar range was catalogued for 1939 with the addition of a special 2-to 3-ton model.

Our Plate 27 shows the smallest model in the 1936 range, the 34D 1½-tonner with a Buda 196 cu in. four-cylinder engine which was rated at 55 bhp at 2,200 rpm out of cylinders measuring $3\frac{5}{8}$ in. $\times$ $4\frac{3}{4}$ in. Three wheelbase lengths were offered – 140 in., 160 in. and 170 in.

LATIL
[28]

In 1931 the Co-operative Wholsesale Society in collaboration with R A Dyson of Liverpool was instrumental in launching a new regular service of bulk milk transport by using trailer tanks specially adapted for running on railway flat wagons.

The system was that the trailer tank would be loaded at the country milk collection depot and then taken by road tractor to a nearby rail siding where it was winched on to a specially fitted railway flat truck. The truck was fitted with power brakes for passenger train working so that the rail part of the journey could be carried out expeditiously. Upon arrival at the railhead near the London milk bottling plant another road tractor would tow the trailer tank off the railway wagon and take it by road to be unloaded at the bottling plant.

The service was successful in that the handling of individual churns was obviated and on the railway only one wagon was necessary in place of the three previously needed. The first glass lined tanks were later added to by those of stainless steel construction, and as the system became more widely known it was taken up by other users and extended to the bulk movement of other commodities including beer and liquid sugar.

In Plate 28 is shown one of the bulk beer tanks owned by the

London, Midland and Scottish Railway Company which was placed on contract with a brewery in 1939 for the overnight movement of beer in bulk from Camden to Glasgow.

The Latil tractor was originally of French design but was produced in Britain from 1932 to 1955, first at Letchworth and later at Ascot. The four wheel drive and four wheel steering layout made it a highly manoeuvrable unit which found great use as a road tractor as well as for shunting duties in docks and railway yards. Suitably adapted it also found use in forestry work and the Traulier, as it was called in Britain, was also fitted with flanged wheels for use as shunting engine in railway yards.

UNION
[29]

There have been several examples of vehicles constructed by an operator for his own particular use and the Union tractor illustrated in Plate 29 is one of these machines. The builders were the Union Cartage Company Limited, a firm in London specialising in the transport of meat.

Meat transporters have found that the drawbar trailer is particularly suited for their purpose because it can be left unattended at docks and markets whilst being loaded or unloaded and the tractor unit can be employed elsewhere. One tractor can be kept busy ferrying trailers to and from the docks if the market is within a few miles or trailers can be taken to the depot area for attaching to other vehicles ready for long distance movements.

The tractors built by Union Cartage took over the duties of some Foden steam tractors which had themselves been adapted from old steam wagons. The Union tractors were the result of a need for some oil engined tractors and were built up from various units, including Foden steam wagon chassis frames, Gardner 5LW engines, Foden or Fowler radiators and other parts fabricated in their own workshops.

Just over forty of the tractors were built during the period 1935–1938, and they could be seen plying their way between Silvertown Docks area and London's Smithfield meat market until about 1965 when Dodge and Scammell tractors took over.

RENAULT
[30]

The range of Renault commercials started just after the turn of the century with a small van modelled on the current private car of the time. The number of models gradually expanded until 1955 when the SAVIEM group was formed and the larger models were then marketed by that group, only the small vans appearing under the Renault title.

In Plate 30 is shown a heavyweight of the 1939 range, the AFKD model which was rated at 11.7 tons gross load capacity. It was of the trailing third axle type of six-wheeler with the chassis frame swept up over the rear axles to give a low centre of gravity, although this design necessitated deep body runners in order to give a uniform platform height. Wheelbase was 4,310 mm, over-all length of chassis 9,740 mm and it was mounted on 10.50 in. × 24 in. tyres all round. A six-cylinder CI engine of 12.5 litres capacity produced 130 bhp and drove through a twin plate clutch and five-speed gearbox with two-speed ranges, to a double reduction axle.

Other vehicles in the range included the following:

AGZ 250 kg van (petrol)
AGS 1,000 kg van (petrol)
AFP 1,500 kg van (petrol)
AGC-L 2,200 kg chassis (petrol)
AGC 2,700 kg van (petrol)
AGP 4,000 kg fc van (petrol or diesel)

AGR 5,500 kg fc chassis (petrol or diesel)
AGK 7 ton fc chassis (petrol or diesel)
AGOD 9.5 ton fc chassis (diesel)

Four-cylinder petrol engines were produced in the following sizes:

58 mm × 95 mm   85 mm × 105 mm   100 mm × 129 mm
120 mm × 130 mm

Diesel engines were a four-cylinder of 100 mm × 150 mm, a four-cylinder of 125 mm × 170 mm and the six-cylinder of 125 mm × 170 mm mentioned above.

TATRA
[31]

Plate 31 shows a truck with a chassis of the most unusual design: the Tatra. With its single large diameter central backbone containing the propeller shaft this layout was the brainchild of Hans Ledwinka and was first used on his Tatra T11 light car of 1923.

The complete design was for a vehicle with central backbone chassis, swinging axles, independent suspension and air cooled engine. Although the vehicle illustrated does not have the latter feature it is worth noting that current Tatra trucks do.

The first swing axle truck was the T13, a 1 litre model of 1924, and in the following year came the first six-wheeler. In 1933 the first diesel engines became available and these were of four-, six- and eight-cylinder types with capacities of 5, 7½ and 10 litres. Later designs included a V12 diesel of 15 litres.

The 27b type illustrated was produced during the 1930s and featured a four-cylinder 4.712 litre water cooled petrol engine which produced 63 bhp at 2,100 rpm from its 100 mm bore × 150 mm stroke cylinders.

WHITE
[32]

The line drawing in Plate 32 shows a type of local delivery van produced by the White Motor Company in 1939. This all steel, integral construction White Horse was built with the convenience of the driver in mind as he carried out his task of making frequent stops to pick up or deliver small items.

To make entry and exit as easy as possible an uncluttered floor is provided which is only 12½ inches from the ground. A small tip-up seat can be used by the driver or the van can be driven from a standing position. Controls consist of the normal steering wheel, a long handbrake lever, a foot brake pedal, a foot operated accelerator which is moved sideways by the foot instead of down, and a T-shaped lever which controls the gear change and clutch.

A four-cylinder horizontally opposed air cooled engine of $3\frac{5}{8}$ in. bore and $3\frac{5}{8}$ in. stroke produces 45 bhp and is mounted below floor level close to the rear axle. The van is of chassisless construction and measures 14 ft $3\frac{5}{8}$ in. on the 104 in. wheelbase and 17 ft $2\frac{1}{4}$ in. on the $121\frac{1}{2}$ in. wheelbase model, 7 ft $5\frac{5}{8}$ in. high and 6 ft 1 in. wide.

VOMAG
[33]

It can be fairly said that the compression ignition engine had its beginnings in Germany, although both Switzerland and Britain were both early on the scene, giving the power unit a thorough testing and rapidly getting it into production and readily accepted.

However great the lead which Germany had at the outset it was soon eroded during the 1930s, not only by foreign competition but also from within. Following upon the general world trade depression of the early thirties and the great swing to National Socialism in Germany, pressure was put upon the German vehicle builders to produce engines which could run easily on fuels which contained a certain percentage of home produced alcohol. This reduced Germany's reliance on imported fuels. Whereas the vehicle building industry would normally have been producing improved designs of CI engines they were being asked to adapt designs to accept producer gas units to run on home produced fuel.

In this respect Germany was not really alone because France, Belgium and to a lesser extent Britain were also spending time and energy testing alternative fuel producing units.

The Vomag chassis illustrated in Plate 33 shows one such system installed by that maker in 1940.

The system used on this 3.5-ton type 3LHG Vomag is typical of those that were being tried out in various parts of Europe at that time. The generator is the large-diameter vertical tank mounted 'on the right just behind the driver's compartment. In the top of this generator the fuel was placed in the shape of wood blocks. As this fuel was burned in a controlled condition it produced carbon monoxide gas and the gas was piped off. It was taken through a cooler to reduce the temperature, through a scrubber to remove impurities and finally to a specially adapted carburettor on the engine. When the gas was mixed with oxygen in the engine cylinder it was ignited by a spark plug as in the usual design of engine using petrol fuel.

In order to conserve load space the cooler and scrubber were placed on the chassis sidemembers and in the Vomag layout an extension was built onto the back of the cab which houses the generator on the right and a fuel bunker on the left.

JNSN
[34]

In many countries the amount of tax payable by the vehicle operator is calculated in proportion to the tare or unladen weight of the vehicle. Therefore any means available for reducing vehicle weight without reducing its strength or carrying capacity is always worth careful study.

During the 1930s the Reynolds Tube Company of Birmingham was faced with the problem of transporting long lengths of their light alloy tubing. Because of the lengths involved, long heavy vehicles had to be employed and this brought another disadvantage: vehicles weighing in excess of $2\frac{1}{2}$ tons were limited to a legal speed of 20 mph.

The first step was to fabricate light alloy bodies using Reynolds light alloys. This did not get rid of the heavy chassis underneath however, so the next step was to produce – in collaboration with Jensen Motors – a lightweight body cum chassis structure to which the running units could be attached.

This Jensen No 1 was designed for a 4-ton payload, used Ford V8 engine and axles, and went into service in February 1939. Unladen weight was 2 tons 6 cwt 2 qrts 10 lbs.

Having accomplished the first vehicle to their satisfaction, the

Company designed No 2 with a longer body in order to handle the longer lengths of tubing being specified by the aircraft industry at that time. It was decided to build the vehicle as a six-wheeler and so gain additional experience. The vehicle was designed to carry 5 tons and Ford running units were again used, but this time the 24 hp four-cylinder engine was installed. When the vehicle was produced in October 1939 the unladen weight was still only 2 tons 9 cwt 2 qtr 17 lbs so it still qualified for the 30 mph speed limit.

Jensen No 3 was built in January 1940 and because of wartime restrictions had to have the floor, cab and sides of wood faced with steel. However the unladen weight even then was only 2 tons 8 cwt 1 qtr 7 lbs.

After the use of these three pilot vehicles during the war years when they covered half a million miles, the postwar range was announced in November 1945. A particularly spacious Luton van was available as well as a drop sided lorry, and in 1947 the articulated Jen-Tug was announced, which was a small-capacity tractor with automatic coupling gear. A battery electric version, the Jen-Helecs, followed later.

In Plate 34 is shown the framework of Jensen No 1 prior to the fitting of the panelling.

ALBION
[35]

The CX 27 twin steer Albion was designed to provide a vehicle which would have a greater carrying capacity than a four-wheeler and yet would be less costly and lighter in weight than the conventional six-wheeler.

Since annual tax was based on the unladen weight of the complete vehicle and regulations limited the weight borne by each axle, Albion's designed this particular chassis for an 11-ton gross load. In this instance gross load was the net payload plus the weight of fitted cab and body. The unladen weight of the complete vehicle including a van body was kept within 5 tons, and by adopting the double front axle layout the rear axle maximum of 8 tons was not exceeded.

The vehicle illustrated in Plate 35 is fitted with a fully insulated body for the conveyance of slaughtered cattle and ran regularly from the West of England to Smithfield meat market in the City of London. Note that the body is fitted with slinging eyes so that it can be lifted by crane if required, although it normally remained bolted to the chassis and was not of the readily detachable type.

Brief Specification
 Wheelbase: 17 ft 4 in.
 Overall length: 26 ft 6 $\frac{1}{2}$ in.
 Overall width: 7 ft 6 in.
 Overall height over cab: 8 ft 4$\frac{1}{2}$ in.
 Turning circle: 66 ft
 Tyre size: 36 in. $\times$ 8 in.
 Albion six-cylinder oil engine 3$\frac{5}{8}$ in. $\times$ 5$\frac{1}{2}$ in. – 105 bhp at
  1,800 rpm
 Dry single plate clutch
 Four-speed gearbox
 Overhead worm rear axle

BEDFORD
[36 and 43]

The first Bedford trucks produced in 1931 were successors to the General Motors Chevrolet built at Hendon in what is now the Frigidaire plant. Production of the Bedford was moved to Luton and the original model – the 2-tonner – was soon added to by the 30-cwt and 12-cwt in 1932.

Wartime production included the popular 3-ton 4 × 4 QL model of which over 50,000 were produced for the armed forces. It was used in many guises including General Service truck, petrol tanker, troop carrier, fire tender and wireless truck. The other popular Bedford models during World War II were the OY 4 × 2 3-tonner and the MW 4 × 2 15-cwt.

At the cessation of hostilities and with the subsequent sales of surplus war vehicles many Bedfords – in common with other ex-military vehicles – were acquired by civilian operators. Many firms took to modifying wartime vehicles to satisfy the great demand for new trucks. Some chassis were completely rebuilt while others were hurriedly pressed into service with little or no change. One British bodybuilder – Neville – produced a cab specifically to convert the OY model into a forward control vehicle and the MW was also available similarly modified.

The QL was particularly useful for transport across unmade country and could be seen at work as a refueller for vehicles engaged on construction sites or as an agricultural lime spreader. It also saw adoption as a recovery vehicle as well as the more ordinary lorry or van. At least one QL front end was mated to a trailer body and frame and saw many years service as a mobile shop, while a forestry contractor succeeded in converting a couple to logging tractors (Plate 43). With the aid of their 4×4 configuration these did good work coupled to a pole trailer hauling logs from forest to saw bench.

Our line drawing in Plate 36 is an elevation of the four stretcher ambulance mounted on the ML 30-cwt chassis for operation by the military in World War II. A similar design of body was also mounted on the Austin K2 chassis and was produced in large numbers by civilian bodybuilders.

The specification for this ambulance called for a seat length of 8 ft 2 in. along either side of the body so that the vehicle could be used for four stretcher or ten sitting cases. A folding seat was provided for the attendant at the front of the body. Double hinged doors and a drop down step were at the rear, while the usual WD fitments for underbody can carriers and a clip for a spade were called for in the specification.

The colour scheme was Khaki Green No 3 (flat) for the body exterior and inside of rear doors, the remainder of the insidebody was Middle Stone BS 62 (glossy). Alternative exterior colours were Mid-Stone or Light Sand for particular theatres of operation.

SCAMMELL
[3, 22, 37, 38, 39, 42, 45 and 117]

'Leeds to London Daily,' 'London to Yorkshire Overnight,' 'London, Birmingham, Manchester and Liverpool' – thus ran the legends on some of the trunk haulage vehicles which nightly set out on their journeys and plied the main routes of Britain prior to 1948.

One company which was well to the fore in providing such regular services was Fisher Renwick Ltd, or Manchester–London Steamers as they were known originally, being coastal shipping owners. With much of their traffic being of a 'smalls' nature (under one hundredweight), a van body was used to a large extent for load protection. For much of their transport Fisher Renwick used Scammells and when they ordered the first rigid eight-wheelers they had them fitted with enormous van bodies. Such was the size of these vehicles that they soon gained he nickname of 'Showboats'. In common with other vehicles in the Fisher Renwick fleet the Scammells were given names instead of the usual fleet numbers allocated to lorries. The Showboats were named after sea birds and in Plate 39 is shown 'Curlew' in its 1940 wartime livery.

Upon the nationalisation of free enterprise transport under the Transport Act 1947 the Fisher Renwick fleet was taken over by the Road Haulage Executive and soon the vehicles were painted green all over with white lettering. The once familiar names of birds, rivers and gods disappeared and even the bodies had the roof line lowered so as to reduce the chance of accident when they were being handled by drivers unfamiliar with their extreme height.

The Scammell R8 chassis was introduced in 1937 and featured a 17 ft 3 in. wheelbase and 29 ft 9 in. overall length. Power was supplied by a Gardner 6LW oil engine and drive was through a Scammell six-speed gearbox to a spiral bevel rear axle with epicyclic final gearing. In true Scammell tradition the rear tyres were of 13.50 × 16 section with 36 × 8 on the front, although options were available.

As well as general haulage vehicles Scammell have produced many different designs of vehicle for cross country and military

127

use and these have gained a reputation for being very versatile vehicles in this specialised field of transport. The 'Pioneer', 'Constructor', 'Mountaineer' and 'Explorer' have found wide acceptance as vehicles particularly suited for oilfield, desert, heavy haulage and cross country conditions. One special type produced in 1935 was the pair of bonnetted 6 × 4 tractors for the Anglo Iranian Oil Company which featured Parsons 160 bhp petrol engines (Plate 22).

Heavy haulage tractors have been another Scammell speciality and two types are shown in Plate 3 and Plate 117. The first is the famous 100-tonner produced in 1929 and the other is the Samson 75-ton tractor of 1970. These two drawings show how the layout of heavy haulage tractors has developed during the period covered in this book.

Two of the 100-ton Scammells were built: the first was KD 9168 which went to Marston's Road Services and the second was originally used in Cornwall and later acquired by Pickfords (BLH 21).

As originally supplied the 100-tonner had a Scammell four-cylinder (5 in. × $5\frac{1}{2}$ in.) petrol engine fitted, but after 3 years it was replaced by a Gardner 6LW diesel engine for greater power. The chassis frame had to be lengthened to accommodate the longer Gardner engine.

The Samson was acquired by Pickfords in 1970 as an experimental eight-wheel heavy tractor and its design took certain features from the current Crusader 6 × 4 tractor. The Samson 8 × 4 unit was designed for a 75-ton gross combination weight and was powered by a General Motors type 8V71N two-stroke V8 diesel of 290 bhp output.

The most familiar types of Scammell in Great Britain have been the 'Mechanical Horse' (Plate 38), the articulated frameless tanker (Plate 45) and the ballasted drawbar tractor (Plate 42), while for use overseas the 'Pioneer' (Plate 37) earned a reputation as a 'go-anywhere' vehicle because of its amazing cross-country abilities.

REO
[40]

With the start of vehicle production during the first ten years of the century the Reo concern launched their famous Speed Wagon

128

in 1915, and the name was used on successive designs up to the 1930s.

The range consisted mainly of trucks in the 30-cwt to 5-ton bracket with a 15-cwt van being introduced in 1938. The majority of the types used six-cylinder petrol engine, dry plate clutch, four-speed gearbox and spiral bevel axle, with a four-cylinder engine for the smallest model during the 1930s.

The outfit shown in Plate 40 is an aviation gasoline tanker which saw service in Britain during World War II when it was used to transport aviation spirit from the Shell Mex and BP terminal at Fulham to US Army Air Force bases.

The tractor is a 29XS model 6 × 6 fitted with Hercules type HXD, six-cylinder 180 bhp petrol engine. The tank semi-trailer is a 4,000-gallon elliptical spirit tank mounted on a stepped frame tandem axle running gear. Where gravity discharge could not be adopted the spirit could be unloaded by means of an engine-driven pump mounted at the rear of the trailer.

DIAMOND T
[41]

Of all the World War II military vehicles which were put into civilian use after the war probably none will outlast the American Diamond T. Many of these are still to be found in Western Europe doing the duty of wreckers, heavy haulage tractors, tippers and tankers, especially for site work.

Diamond T produced the 969 model as the basis for a wrecker and the 980 and 981 as a heavy haulage tractor for drawbar trailer operation in connection with tank transport and recovery.

The 969 was a 6 × 6 bonnetted vehicle with a wheelbase of 151 in. and an overall length of 291½ in. It was fitted with a Hercules RXC six-cylinder petrol engine of 592 cu in. displacement which produced 106 bhp at 2,300 rpm. A twin boom Holmes wrecking crane was fitted.

Model 980 and 981 tractors were of 6 × 4 type and were produced from 1941 to 1945 originally for the British forces primarily for the transport of military tanks on trailers. The tractor had a wheelbase of 179¼ in. and measured 280 in. overall, and was powered by a Hercules DFXE six-cylinder diesel engine developing 185 bhp at 1,600 rpm.

As mentioned above many Diamond T six-wheelers found their way into the hands of civilian operators after the war and Pickfords, the well known British heavy haulage specialists, were lucky enough to have them for tank transport before the end of the war as heavy haulage tractors. A pair of these vehicles are shown in Plate 41 moving a large boiler in 1947.

PACIFIC
[44]

One particular type of vehicle which has been dear to the hearts of heavy haulage enthusiasts in Britain is the ex-American Army Pacific tractor. Several of these were acquired by Robert Wynn and Son of Newport, Monmouthshire and used for a variety of heavy haulage tasks throughout the country.

Wynn's rebuilt the tractors to their own requirements and converted them from articulated units into ballasted drawbar tractors. For the twenty years or so after World War II these powerful tractors could be seen handling the largest and heaviest of tasks all over Britain. One was later rebuilt a second time while another was equipped as a recovery vehicle.

The tractors started life as the prime mover portion of a US Army articulated tank transporter (designated M25). They were produced by the Pacific Car and Foundry Company – type TR1 – and were originally fitted with armoured cabs but later types were of normal materials. A Hall Scott six-cylinder 1,090 cu in. petrol engine producing 240 bhp at 2,000 rpm was the original fitment. Wheelbase was 172 in. A Knuckey rear bogie with chain drive was an unusual feature but the front axle was shaft driven.

In use with Wynn's the tractors had Cummins NHRS6B six-cylinder diesel engines fitted. They often worked in tandem or were coupled at either end of the trailer being handled. Our Plate 44 shows 'Dreadnought' while at work in 1955 moving a giant electrical stator for the English Electric Company.

In addition to the Pacifics, Wynn's were users of other military equipment including Diamond T heavy haulage tractors and FWD CU type 4 × 4 timber tractors designed for use with logging trailers in the Welsh hillside forests.

FIAT
[46]

The name FIAT (originally Fabbrica Italiana Automobili Torino and later Fiat) has become synonymous with the motor vehicle of Italy. This giant of the world's motor industry started producing commercials in 1903 and since then the range has gradually been extended to take in all sizes from the commercial version of the diminutive '500' car with a carrying capacity of 300 kg up to six-wheel tractor units and four-axle rigid chassis for maximum capacity loads.

Plate 46 shows a model from the range of the late 1940s which is a 666N trailer model fitted with a six-cylinder diesel engine of 120 mm bore × 138 mm stroke which produced 105 bhp. Drive was through a single dry plate clutch and short shaft to an eight-speed gearbox mounted separately, thence by open propellor shaft to a double reduction spiral bevel axle.

The vehicle was of 3,850 mm wheelbase and measured 7,070 mm overall, and was carried on 1,050 × 20 tyres.

In common with many other European countries Italy found great use with drawbar trailers for long distance haulage. The trailer of the outfit depicted in our plate is of the self steering rear axle type, that is to say both axles of the trailer are connected so that they turn in opposite directions. As the leading axle of the trailer is pulled to the left by the towing vehicle so the connecting rods beneath the trailer move the rear axle on the opposite lock. This gives the trailer better 'tracking' characteristics on tight turns such as would be found on mountain hairpin bends. Another feature of many Italian (and Swiss) vehicles is the provision of right hand steering so that the driver can keep better observation of the right hand road edge when operating in mountainous regions with their dangerous sheer drops.

PROCTOR
[47]

Following World War II there was a desperate shortage of new vehicles available in Britain and Europe, and the ex-military units were seized upon as soon as they were available at the auctions. Some were used in their wartime guise for many years while others were rebuilt almost completely and were in use for 25 years and more.

In Britain operators were anxious for new vehicles and in addition to the large producers several smaller firms helped fill the void left by five years of war.

In the light vehicle class vans by Jowett (Plate 53) and Trojan helped with local deliveries while Rutland (Plate 63) and Jensen (Plate 54) were available in the middleweight 5/6-ton load size.

Another contender in those early postwar years was the Proctor (Plate 47). This was a 5/6-tonner built by Proctor Spring-wood Ltd of Mousehold, Norwich and later by Praill's Motors Ltd of Hereford. Production was limited to the 1947–1952 period.

There were three models in the range, the 6-ton Mark 1, a 13 ft $8\frac{1}{2}$ in. wheelbase model for general haulage or van work, the $7\frac{1}{2}$-ton Mark 2 with 9 ft 9 in. wheelbase for operation as a tipper, and the 10-ton Mark 3 tractor chassis with 8 ft wheelbase and Scammell automatic coupling gear.

All models had the Perkins P6 oil engine (70 bhp at 2,200 rpm) driving through a single dry plate clutch and David Brown 5-speed gearbox to a spiral bevel rear axle.

MACK
[48]

The first Mack trucks date from 1905 under the name Manhattan and these included 2-ton and 5-ton types. Other sizes were added to the catalogue as time went on and they were of similar style, having four-cylinder engines, cone clutches and three-speed gear-boxes. During the first few years of production both 'cab over' and conventional bonnetted layout were offered.

In 1911 the International Motor Company was formed which controlled both Mack and Saurer in America; a little later Hewitt was acquired.

World War I came and with it came orders for Mack trucks for Europe. A lot of the Mack reputation came from the use of the legendary Bulldog, with its coal-scuttle front end, in the European war, when many thousands of this AC model were sent across the Atlantic.

The company changed its name to Mack Trucks Inc in 1922 and during the 1920s production was expanded, mostly with the AB and AC models but later in the decade new models were added – the AK, AL and AP, as well as the BB, BC, BG, BJ and BL. The thirties saw the reintroduction of the coe types after a lapse of many years and a growing number of six-wheelers and truck trailer types were being sold.

It is not only the early Mack AC model which is noted for for strength. Many other Mack trucks have been used for long periods as various models used in World War II still bear witness.

In Plate 48 is shown an LM Mack six-wheeler of the 1940s which was still being operated on international haulage in 1973! The operator of this vehicle really does mean international when he says it; this truck was seen in London waiting for a return load to Iran after arriving from Holland. It had travelled through Turkey, Greece, Bulgaria, Yugoslavia, Italy, Switzerland, France and Belgium to deliver its load, a real tribute to the faith the operator and his driver have in this vehicle.

GMC
[49]

In Plate 49 is shown an American GMC 'doubles' outfit – the name given to a combination consisting of tractor, semi-trailer and full trailer.

This type of combination first came into use during the 1930s and has gradually spread to 33 of the north American states. Lesgislation in each State prescribes the limitations placed upon the operation of such outfits by means of maximum length, axle weights, gross weights, etc, as well as listing the roads or routes upon which the operation of doubles is permissible. The majority of States allowing the operation of doubles place a 65 ft maximum length limit on them with just a few allowing 70 ft. A handful of others are more restrictive, having 55 feet as their maximum – a stringent law rendering the operation of such outfits almost useless.

In practice it has been found that to operate a doubles outfit consisting of two 25 or 27 ft trailers allows a much greater degree of flexibility in operation than to use the same tractor pulling a single 40-ft trailer. Operators have found that large semi-trailers are often not used to capacity unless held over for an additional consignment, which can result in having to make two separate deliveries. With doubles one trailer can be dropped off at an intermediate point for unloading while the other is taken further on.

Another point made by operators is that temperature control is easier with the shorter 25-ft trailers than with the longer trailers, an important point when handling perishables in varying ambient temperature conditions at different times of the year.

One drawback of the doubles outfit is its higher first cost, but this is more than offset by the additional running time achieved by two shorter trailers because of a reduction in turn-round time. Although there will be more trailers in a fleet for a given carrying capacity the greater operational efficiency obtainable with a greater number of units offsets the proportionately higher capital outlay.

Although a few other countries allow the operation of doubles the system has so far not found favour in Britain, though a few demonstrations have been done by trailer builders on private roads. Supporters of the system on this side of the Atlantic realise that the use of such outfits would have to be limited to certain roads and routes and that areas where the combination could be split into two normal articulated outfits would have to be found. These are relatively minor problems, and as an indication of the acceptance of such an idea one has only to look at the progress made in the United States over the past forty years. There doubles outfits up to 98 ft in length are allowed on certain turnpikes, while in a few cases an additional trailer has been added to the combination, so making it into a 'triple'. The problem of sufficient power for such an operation is met by the provision of a powerful 'dolly' in the combination.

MAUDSLAY
[50]

A very early starter in vehicle building, the Maudslay Motor Company was set up in 1904, and private cars were produced until 1926.

By 1928 the range of lorries consisted of four models: the C3-4, a 3/4-tonner with four-cylinder engine of $4\frac{1}{2}$ in. $\times$ 6 in., the C4-5, a heavier version of the 3-4 with engine of $4\frac{3}{4}$ in. $\times$ 6 in., and the C7-8 which was again a more heavily constructed chassis with the same sized engine.

In 1929 the L type with five payload variations replaced the C model, and in 1930 a 10-ton six-wheeler – the L10 – was added to the range. This model was powered by a four-cylinder (5 in. $\times$ 6 in.) petrol engine of 75 bhp and measured 24 ft 6 in. overall. A four-speed gearbox and bevel gear axle was fitted, and the chassis was available on either solid rubbers or 40 in. $\times$ 8 in. pneumatics.

By 1932 the 3 and 4-ton models had been dropped from the range and the six-wheeler was now uprated to 12 tons. The solid rubbers had been discontinued.

1934 saw the first oil engined lorry offered – the 6-ton Six-four which sold for £1,185 in chassis form – £310 more than the petrol version. By 1937 six oil engined types were available – Six-four $7\frac{1}{2}$-ton), LL1 (5-ton), LL3 (4/5-ton), L10-5, a 10-ton six-wheeler. SW, a 13-ton six-wheeler and EW, a 15-ton eight-wheeler.

The use of model names had begun in 1932 for the passenger chassis but it was not until 1938 that the goods vehicles became known by names such as 'Mogul', 'Maharanee', 'Mikado', etc. These type names fitted in very well with the AEC range when Maudslay became part of the ACV Group in 1948, and after a short while the Maudslay products disappeared and AEC vehicles with Maudslay badges were marketed. The old Maudslay name of 'Mogul' was revived for a bonnetted export tractor built at the Maudslay works, and as recent as 1973 a Leyland 'Marathon' tractor appeared, this name having previously graced the Maudslay 36 seat passenger chassis of 1938/39.

In Plate 50 is shown an ACV type of Maudslay of the early 1950s. This is a model 3817M 'Meritor' in use by British Road Services. Of particular interest is the open top van body specially designed for the transport of woollen goods from Yorkshire. This design allowed the vehicle to be loaded from above, and after loading a canvas sheet was tied across the top to protect the load. Double hinged doors and tailboard were used at the rear.

BROWN
[51]

Plate 51 shows a 1950 Brown tractor, one of about 1,000 which were built during the period 1939–1953.

The Brown tractor was the brainchild of J L Brown, the Chief Engineer of Horton Motor Lines, Charlotte, North Carolina. He reckoned that the trucking company could build a better tractor than that being produced commercially in the late 1930s.

So in 1939 the first four-wheeled conventional appeared. These first models were made up of Parish frames, Continental petrol engines and a Fuller transmission, but during the fourteen years of production Buda and Cummins diesel engines were also fitted.

Following a merger of Hortons and six other trucking companies into Associated Transport in 1942 the Browns appeared in a new livery and at the end of the war the cab-over model 513 was introduced. In 1948 this model was offered for sale to other trucking lines but as it was hand built and expensive few were sold outside the Associated group. Production ceased in 1953 when it was found more economical to purchase proprietary tractors.

AUSTIN
[52]

During the past twenty years or so a lot of thought has gone into the design of an ideal vehicle for collection and delivery work. For

136

many years motor bodywork designs had changed very little from their horsedrawn forebears and when the Austin 3-Way van was announced in 1948 it showed that considerable thought had gone into its design (Plate 52).

The underlying concept was that the vehicle should provide a high degree of accessibility to the load in order to make the driver's lot easier. Most local delivery vehicles of the day had access to the load mainly from the rear with perhaps a slim opening alongside the driver, whereas the '3-Way' gave good access on three sides.

Designed to carry a 25-cwt payload within a 300 cu ft body-space, it had double hinged doors at either side and at the rear. A fully forward cab contained the engine over the front axle and single 32×6 tyres all round caused minimum intrusion to the loadspace.

Theoretically the design was a good one and many saw service with shops and traders involved with delivery work. The payload was a little small, as perhaps the body was for a full day's deliveries, but nevertheless it marked an important contribution toward the ideal local delivery vehicle.

Many other vehicles have appeared with a similar aim in mind, such as the Dennis 'Stork' and 'Paravan', Thames 'Clearway', Commer 'WalkThru', Bedford Hawson, Morris Commercial J and PV, BMC 'EA' and many other bodywork designs giving much greater access through the use of roller shutters or canvas curtains. A popular American delivery van was the Divco shown in Plate 71, while many battery electric vehicles have appeared on the delivery van market, although none quite reaches the standard of accessibility coupled with security of the Austin '3-Way'.

JOWETT BRADFORD
[53]

The Jowett Bradford was the postwar model of these light van builders, who were well know for their light cars which embodied an engine design largely unchanged over thirty years.

137

The original Jowett vans were produced from 1925 onward and in common with other light vans of the period were adaptations of private car chassis. The power unit was a 2-cylinder horizontally opposed unit of 7 hp (75.4×101.5), driving through a 3-speed gearbox to a bevel rear axle. During the 1930s the design was gradually improved with the load capacity going from 4 cwt to 5 cwt, to 7 cwt, to 8 cwt and finally a 10-cwt model in 1934.

After the war three basic models were announced with the introduction of the Bradford name (the Jowett factory was at Bradford, Yorkshire). They were a van, a light truck and a personnel carrier.

The CB model, rated at 5 cwt, was advertised from 1948. This had the usual 2-cylinder horizontally opposed engine and three-speed gearbox driving to a spiral bevel rear axle. The gearbox had top gear position located at the bottom left hand of the the gate with the result that the poor little engine took a hiding from inexperienced drivers who persisted in pulling away from rest in top gear. The CC model introduced later had the more orthodox gearbox layout which helped matters no end. Plate 53 shows one of this type produced in 1951.

With the shortage of new vehicles in the early postwar years the Bradford van sold quite well but as the small vans produced by Ford, Austin, Commer and Morris became more plentiful the little Jowett was squeezed out, perhaps because of its unorthodox design. The Jowett Javelin and Jupiter cars of the same period are fast becoming collectors' items and one wonders if perhaps a few Bradfords might also bathe in their reflected glory?

GUY
[54]

Guy Motors started in 1914 with the production of a 15.9 hp 30-cwt chassis with 11 ft 5 in. wheelbase, four-cylinder (80 mm $\times$ 130 mm) engine, four-speed gearbox and double reduction rear axle. A 2-ton model (type B) was introduced in 1915, and the BA in 1921. From 1922 onwards the range was gradually extended from the six models of that year (15-cwt to 3-ton) to eight lorry models (25-cwt to 7-ton) and eleven bus models in 1928.

In 1934 diesel engines were offered in the 4-ton TD model, 'Warrior' 6½-tonner and 'Goliath' 11-tonner, while in the following year models as small as the CFS 2-tonner could be fitted with an oil engine at extra cost.

In the late 1930s the range extended from the 'Wolf' CF type 2-tonner to a 7-ton oiler with a 12-ton articulated unit. However, Guy produced mostly in the medium weight range, with a great part of their output in the 2-ton to 5-ton payload classes with the 'Wolf', 'Vixen' and 'Otter' models.

Wartime production consisted of 4×2 and 4×4 15-cwt trucks, 4×4 gun tractors and a few civilian vehicles for supply against Ministry of Transport permits.

The early postwar range included three medium weight models until the mid 1950s when a heavier range was announced. Originally designated the 'Goliath', after an earlier range, the model name was quickly changed to 'Invincible' in order to avoid confusion with a German vehicle of similar title.

Four-, six- and eight-wheel chassis were included in the range, and Plate 54 shows one of the latter type. The chassis bore a great similarity to the current AEC 'Mammoth Major', using as it did many AEC components.

AEC·
[55,113]

In Plate 55 is pictured an AEC 'Mammoth Major Mark III' tanker being reversed aboard the British Railways cross-channel ferry at Dover in 1951. The carrying of this tanker marked a new departure for its owners because beer destined for the bottling plant in Belgium had been shipped at first in wooden casks and later in demountable tanks, which had to be craned on and off the ships. The tank was of 2,880 gallons capacity and was made of stainless steel with two inches of Alfol insulation added, and the whole cladded with aluminium.

The 'Mammoth Major' chassis was the largest of a range of goods vehicles manufactured by AEC, and the eight-wheel Mark

III was the postwar version of the Mark II which was originally introduced in 1934.

In original form the 16 ft 10½ in. mean wheelbase chassis (18 ft 6½ in. alternative) was available with either the AEC six-cylinder (110 × 130) petrol engine developing 120 bhp at 2,400 rpm or the AEC six-cylinder (115 × 142) oil engine which developed 130 bhp at 2,400 rpm. Drive was by single plate clutch, four-speed main gearbox and two-speed auxiliary gearbox to a double reduction rear axle. The fourth axle was of the trailing type. Tyre size was 40 in. × 8 in.

In postwar Britain the Mammoth Major re-appeared in March 1945 in limited numbers but with the 7.7-litre (105 mm × 146 mm) engine. The new 9.6-litre engine (120 mm × 142 mm) which produced 125 bhp was announced in September 1945 and was designed for use in the Mammoth Major six- and eight-wheelers.

The Mark III was available in two mean wheelbase lengths of 14 ft 6½ in. and 18 ft 9½ in. and was designed for operation at 22 tons gross. The clutch was of the dry single plate type, a five-speed gearbox was fitted and both single and double drive rear axles were offered. The single drive was of double reduction spiral bevel type while the double drive bogie was of overhead worm type.

Following the introduction of lightweight, high volume van trailers and the gradual swing to articulated vehicles during the 1960s, the rigid eight-wheel chassis was gradually toppled from its premier position as the epitome of the British trunk vehicle.

The demand for a versatile, heavy tractor unit to handle the long-distance runs was met by the Mandator, and a drawing of this type is shown in Plate 113 which depicts a 9 ft 6 in. wheelbase version with Ergomatic tilt cab which was fitted to the model as from 1964.

FBW
[56]

Plate 56 shows a plan and elevational drawing of a model L40V FBW truck of the 1950s period.

This vehicle is designed for a six-ton payload and is powered by the DD type six-cylinder oil engine of 110 mm bore × 150 mm stroke which produces 110 bhp.

Many Swiss vehicles are designed for use with a trailer, and the FBW has a towing jaw and air brake connections fitted at the rear end as standard. Trailer operation in such mountainous regions requires adequate power, and in order to keep the engine to an economical size the FBW is fitted with a two-speed auxiliary gearbox in addition to the normal four-speed gearbox. This auxiliary gearbox which doubles the speed range of the ordinary gearbox is situated midway along the chassis and is air operated.

The chassis frame is somewhat unusual in that it is high enough to clear the rear axle at the rear end while it sweeps down at a point just in front of the rear axle and continues at the low level to the front. This design gives a wide gap between chassis frame and body toward the front but does permit a low cab line.

Other models in the range at this period included $4\frac{1}{2}$- and 7-ton trucks and 4-, $5\frac{1}{2}$- and $6\frac{1}{2}$-ton tippers. Three engine types were fitted: RD 4-cylinder (110 × 150) producing 70 bhp; the 6-cylinder DD mentioned above, and the 6-cylinder ED (125 × 150) which was rated at 145 bhp.

COMMER
[57]

Illustrated in Plate 57 is a 1953 Commer 10-ton articulated outfit operated by J W Green Ltd, brewers of Luton, Bedfordshire. The tractor is a 7 ft 9 in. wheelbase unit and is powered by the Commer 4750 cc six-cylinder petrol engine which produces 109 bhp at 3000 rpm.

This model in the Commer range was first introduced in 1948 with the six-cylinder petrol engine, but after the Rootes Group had acquired Tilling Stevens in 1953 it was possible to use that company's revolutionary three-cylinder opposed piston diesel engine as an alternative. This 3261 cc two-stroke power unit was available as from 1954.

The Commer TS3 engine, as it was called, used pressure charging from a Rootes type blower, and ran best at near its maximum speed of 2400 rpm. Liked by drivers for its lively performance, it does however produce a distinctly loud exhaust bark.

The trailer of the J W Green outfit was built by Hands Trailers and has some unusual features. The design has a pleasant rounded, almost streamlined shape which satisfies appearance rather than capacity. A sliding roof is provided and this gave light and ventilation for the loaders in the pre palletised era. A roller shutter enclosed the rear.

Because of the low loading nature of the vehicle a stepped frame was utilised and some of the load was carried on the swan neck. When the time came for replacement the trailers were ousted by a fleet of York 'Freightmaster' vans embodying Joloda channels for pallet handling. A couple of the old Hands trailers were then relegated to operation as mobile bars for use at outside functions, after the necessary modification.

BRISTOL
[58]

The name of Bristol goes back to 1908 when the first vehicles were produced by the Bristol Tramways and Carriage Company. During the early part of its history Bristol produced mostly passenger chassis and from 1931 onwards no lorry chassis were offered.

Because of their obvious connections with the passenger transport industry the company became a member of the Tilling Group in 1938 and their famous K and L model passenger chassis were a familiar sight in the large bus undertakings of the Tilling Group.

It was a short step from the large bus operating companies to the nationalised bus undertakings and after the 1947 Transport Act Bristol set about building buses for the nationalised operators only.

In 1952 a great new step was taken when Bristol produced a design for a rigid eight-wheel lorry chassis for the Road Haulage Executive. The thinking behind the production of such a vehicle was that the national road transport undertaking, British Road

Services should follow the lead of the bus side and buy its vehicles from within.

The HG chassis was of 18 ft 0 in. mean wheelbase, 29 ft 10 in. overall. A Leyland 0.600 six-cylinder diesel engine of 9819 cc (122 × 140) was fitted and the drive taken through a five-speed gearbox to a double reduction third axle with trailing fourth axle. Tyre size was 36 in. × 8 in., and the unladen weight with Eastern Coachworks cab (another company within the British Transport Commission) and platform body was $7\frac{1}{4}$ tons.

Some years later a tractor version of the Bristol was produced in order to meet the gradual changeover to articulation in the BRS fleet. This model had the Leyland 0.680 engine fitted.

Following a change of Government the Transport Act 1953 made provision for parts of the BRS fleet to be sold off to private enterprise and eventually some of the Bristol vehicles passed into the hands of private hauliers. Plate 58 shows one of the rigid eight-wheelers which was operated by Cusick and Company on trunk haulage work with a drawbar trailer.

KENWORTH
[59]

Plate 59 shows one of the most unusual heavy haulage tractors in use today, an early postwar ex-American Army model M249 tank transporter tractor. A pair of these powerful 4 × 4s are currently used by Les Transports Jonet of Charleroi, Belgium for heavy haulage movements up to 360,000 pounds gross. Powered by Cummins NTK335 diesel engines driving through Allison semi-automatic gearboxes, these Kenworths have other transatlantic stablemates, notably Diamond T, Pacific, Federal and Autocar – a sure indication of the high regard paid to American trucks by Belgian operators.

The current line of Kenworths includes conventional and coe models with day cabs or sleepers, four wheels or tandems for over-the-road or off-highway use. In fact Kenworth trucks are custom built to the user's specification in the heavy duty ranges.

There is the PD series named the 'Hustler' which with its forward control cab is the medium weight model in the range, and is designed for inter-city use.

The W-900 series is the conventional model available with a wide choice of engine, power train and axle options, while the LW924 model was originally designed as a tractor for the logging and mining industries. It is now widely used in the construction industry as a 14 cu yd dumper or 10 cu yd truckmixer.

The 'Brute' is a chassis designed to take a 13 cu yd mixer or 16 cu yd dump body and can be obtained as conventional tandem or tridem axle layout. The C520 is a long wheelbase truck designed for use in States with weight restrictions on certain bridges which precludes the use of conventional types.

For off-highway use Kenworth produces a wide range of chassis of 4 $\times$ 4, 6 $\times$ 4 and 6 $\times$ 6 layout which have Cummins NHC250, NH230 and NTC335 engines, or Detroit Diesel 12V – 71N65 two-strokes as alternatives.

COLEMAN-MARMON HERRINGTON
[60]

Marmon Herrington have become famous as the company specialising in the conversion of motor chassis to all wheel drive. Large producers of trucks find it uneconomical to produce 4 $\times$ 4 vehicles for the limited demand which exists as opposed to that for conventional rear-driven machines. This is the market catered for by specialist builders such as Marmon Herrington, who have a particular niche in modern truck production.

Although 4 $\times$ 4 conversions are produced mainly for Dodge and Ford, various other types appear similarly modified. The wing type snow plough shown in Plate 60 is a Marmon Herrington conversion of a short-wheelbase Coleman truck operated by the Colorado Highway Department for road maintenance work. This 1954 model has a tipping body for carrying sand, salt or road aggregate and behind the cab a small hydraulic crane is mounted for loading heavy items of highway furniture.

Marmon Herrington have also produced normal over-the-road tractors and a wide range of special vehicles including scout cars, armoured trucks and wreckers for the military.

ALFA ROMEO
[61]

Better known for their sports cars, Alfa Romeo started producing commercials in 1930 and continued to do so until about 1970. The more recent vehicles included vehicles built under licence from SAVIEM, and a small forward control van called the Romeo.

During the 1960s the range was called the 'Mille' and with the 11-litre engine fitted an unladen vehicle must have had a performance quite befitting the Alfa name.

Plate 61 shows a vehicle from the Mille range. This is the normal wheelbase truck version. The vehicle has a wheelbase of 3,660 mm and an overall length of 7,135 mm, while the tractor version was only 6,405 mm overall but had a wheelbase similar to that of the truck model.

A six-cylinder diesel engine of 125 mm bore × 150 mm stroke produced 178 bhp at 2,000 rpm from its swept volume of 11,050 cc and drove through a dual range four-speed gearbox which gave a total of eight forward and two reverse speeds. The truck was designed to operate at a gross vehicle weight of 35,273 lbs, while the trailer model was rated at 44,092 lbs gtw.

DOUGLAS
[62]

With the increase in recent years in the number of vehicle carrying ferries there has grown up a need for special tractors which can handle all types of trailers with ease of mobility.

On ferries that have a loading ramp at one end only, a fair amount of manoeuvring has to take place and this can be costly because of delays in turn-round time.

The Douglas 'Tugmaster' is one such design of shunting tractor which has been produced to match the need for a highly mobile unit for dockside work. This company has had many years of experience in producing specialist vehicles such as yard shunters, aircraft towing tractors, logging vehicles, railway shunting tractors, fire fighting vehicles and special vehicles for loading aircraft.

Naturally one model for handling all shunting needs is not possible so the company offer options with regard to such items as wheelbase, engine, gearbox, transmission, cab design, coupling gear and handling facilities.

The NS/8 type shown in Plate 62 is typical of the type used for handling semi-trailers of the normal size. It is fitted with a 105 bhp CI engine, has 8 forward and 2 reverse speeds, a double reduction rear axle, and vacuum and air pressure systems for handling most types of trailers. The wheelbase of this tractor is considerably longer than normal road tractors so that trailers with a set back king pin can be handled, and an important feature is the fifth wheel which can be raised hydraulically so that trailer landing gear is clear of the ground for quick turn-round of trailers at the dockside.

MOTOR TRACTION
[63]

Motor Traction Ltd was a small concern which turned out hand built lorry chassis, mostly for export. Production commenced in 1947 with prototypes and after about three years trials were announced to the public.

The phrase 'composite vehicle' was used to describe the products of the works which was situated at Croydon in Surrey. This description was used in order to convey the Company's belief that a vehicle was only as good as the components from which it was made. Therefore by using running units such as engines, gearboxes and axles which had already stood the test of time and were well known and trusted for the name they bore, they hoped to produce a vehicle which would become equally good. By using proprietary units and using them within their capabilities they would create a good vehicle provided that all the components were properly matched and compatible with one another.

So we find that included in the specification of the chassis produced were engines by Leyland, Perkins, Gardner and Meadows, axles by Kirkstall or Eaton, brakes by Girling and gearboxes by David Brown.

146

The man behind the design of both Rutland and MTN chassis (Rutland was the name used for the UK and Commonwealth vehicles, while MTN was for markets in Spain, South America and Pakistan) was Frank Manton who had followed his father in the motor trade. Before World War II there was quite a lot of conversion work done on Commer and Albion chassis by adding axles and generally rebuilding them with CI engines. These vehicles went under the name of Manton.

During the years of production up to 1958 quite a number of designs were produced, and naturally with a small volume of production it was possible to introduce items to suit individual specifications. However, included in the range were the following:

Albacore: a 6-ton payload chassis

Albatross: a 6/7-tonner

Condor: 8-ton six-wheeled chassis

Eagle: heavy duty 8-ton chassis

Falcon: a 4/5-ton chassis

Minor 4: 3/4-ton chassis

Minor 6: 2/3-ton chassis

Stuka: a later version of the Albatross but with single speed axle.

Troubadour: 8-ton four-wheeler with Perkins R6, and with normal control

Tucan: a 5/6-ton chassis

There were also 4 × 4, 6 × 4 and crane carrier chassis produced for special orders.

The vehicle shown in Plate 63 is a twin steer version of the Stuka.

Possibly the best summary of the vehicles produced by Motor Traction, and the thinking behind their design, is contained in a paragraph from one of the brochures. It says . . . 'The basic design and layout is our responsibility, to which we apply our skill and experience, and to this can be added the advantage of integrating units produced by the Specialist limiting his concentration in one direction rather than over an extended field'.

NORDE
[64]

In Britain there were many spokesmen in favour of a national motor road system long before the start of the ambitious *auto-*

bahnen scheme in Germany. However, it was to take a very long time for the British road system to get under way and it was not until 1958 that the first true motor road was opened, albeit just a length of 8.26 miles skirting Preston in Lancashire.

Unlike the German, the British network did not progress at a rate that could be called alarming, and similarly there was no violent change in vehicle design as there had been at the Berlin Shows during the 1930s.

The M1 motorway extended for approximately 70 miles when opened in 1959 and a few vehicles did appear which could cover its length in just over the hour. One of these was the Norde articulated outfit (Plate 64) which was constructed by North Derbyshire Engineering Ltd for Toft Brothers and Tomlinson, hauliers of Matlock, Derbyshire.

The long-wheelbase tractor unit with Bowyer cab had a turbocharged Cummins 262 bhp engine installed with fluid flywheel and Wilson 8-speed semi-automatic gearbox. Mounted on 40 in. × 8 in. tyres the vehicle was capable of 70 mph and returned a fuel consumption of around $6\frac{1}{2}$ mpg on the motorway.

Norde hit the headlines again in 1962 when another revolutionary vehicle was produced. This time it was a lightweight rigid six-wheeler with Bedford TK style cab. As with the tractor chassis rubber suspension was used, a feature which Norde expanded upon by offering their designs to other manufacturers later. This time the power unit was the widely used Perkins 6.354.

TVW
[65]

At the cessation of Sentinel diesel vehicle production around 1956 many of the remaining parts were bought by Transport Vehicles (Warrington) Ltd who set about producing a range of vehicles of their own.

Announced in 1958, the range consisted of three vehicles: a four-wheel tractor unit, a six-wheel and an eight-wheel rigid chassis.

The tractor unit was a 9 ft 0 in. wheelbase chassis and measured 13 ft overall. It was powered with a Rootes TS3 3-cylinder opposed piston two-stroke oil engine driving through a David

148

Brown 557 five-speed gearbox to a Kirkstall overhead worm axle. Unladen weight was approximately 3.5 tons.

The six-wheel chassis also used the TS 3 engine but drove through a Meadows 5-speed overdrive gearbox to a Kirkstall axle. Wheelbase was 15 ft 6 in. with an overall length of 27 ft 6 in. The third axle was of the trailing type and the chassis/cab had an unladen weight of 4 tons 7 cwt.

The rigid eight-wheeler used the Gardner 6LW engine driving through a David Brown 557 main gearbox and two-speed auxiliary box to the Kirkstall worm axle. With a wheelbase of 18 ft, the overall length was 30 ft and unladen weight of chassis/cab was 6.25 tons.

Plate 65 shows one of the eight-wheelers as a high-sided tipper for the transport of coke from the Midlands to London. The extra high body sides are necessary to enable the vehicle to carry its maximum payload of 16.25 tons within the legal gross weight of 24 tons.

DENNIS
[66]

The Dennis range for 1928 consisted of models ranging in capacity from 30 cwts to 6 tons, all powered by four-cylinder petrol engines of 2,725, 4,714, or 5,704 cc capacity. Chassis prices varied from £315 to £860.

A similar range was offered for 1929, but in 1930 a six-cylinder OHC engine of 5,324 cc was produced to power the new 'Arrow' passenger chassis and this unit was utilised for a brand new 12-ton capacity rigid six-wheeler which was offered at a chassis price of £1,425.

During the 1930s the range was improved by the introduction of the 'Lancet', Dennis-Lanova oil engine, Dennis '0' type oil engine, 40/45 cwt with spiral bevel rear axle (as opposed to the normal Dennis worm axle), an articulated eight-wheeler, the light 4-tonner, and 'Ajax' and 'Max' chassis. From just 9 models in 1928 to 28 in 1938 was the achievement of Dennis Brothers and that was not the whole story. In addition to the lorry range there were special municipal vehicles such as gulley emptiers and fire engines which came in a variety of types and sizes. Actually

Dennis gained a lot of custom from the fact that they were willing to build almost any vehicle to customers' requirements, a facility which was to continue right through to the end of lorry production at Guildford.

War production centred on the 5-ton and 'Max' types as far as goods vehicles were concerned but many thousands of trailer fire pumps, Churchill tanks and bren gun carriers kept the works busy during World War II.

Postwar types included the popular 'Pax' 5-tonner, 'Max' 8-tonner and 'Jubilant' 12-ton rigid six-wheeler. A tractor version of the 5-tonner was the 'Horla', designed for single axle semi-trailers with Scammell type automatic coupling gear.

During the 1950s expansion of the range took place by the introduction of models of varying capacity aimed at specific markets. These included the Centaur, Dragon, Hefty, Condor, Heron, Triton, Stork, Vendor and the Paravan. This last model was interesting in that it was a van completely designed with the parcel collection and delivery service in mind. In fact one independent parcel carrier, Essex Carriers, helped considerably in the design of the vehicle. Plate 66 shows the second vehicle when it was announced to the public in August 1958. The vehicle was designed for a 3-ton payload, had a wheelbase of 11 ft 9 in., overall length of 22 ft 6¾ in., overall width of 6 ft 9 in. and a capacity of 600 cu ft.

It will be noticed that the driver's entrance is at the front corner, with a step height of 1 ft 6¼ in., and the door is of an unusual four piece type moving up and over, with a normal roller shutter at the rear of the body.

The Perkins P4 four-cylinder engine of 3.15 litres capacity was mounted above the front axle and the driver had access to the body interior along a walkway beside the engine cover.

KAELBLE
[67]

Karl Kaelble began building vehicles in 1925 and since that time they have turned out many varying types although few of them have been of the common truck type.

Steam, petrol and oil power have been used to power Kaelble

vehicles and they have included agricultural tractors, road tractors, dumpers, heavy haulage tractors, traction engines, heavy lorries and special low loading vehicles.

Road tractors have formed the main part of the company's output and these have been of 4 × 2, 4 × 4, 6 × 2, 6 × 4 and 6 × 6 layout. During the 1930s some unusual tractors were built in collaboration with the Wumag trailer concern. These were of ultra-low loading design and consisted of a framework trailer fitted with rails for the transport of loaded railway wagons.

Plate 67 shows a Kaelble road tractor for towing one or two trailers. Road tractors such as this became very popular in Germany during the 1930s because the government of the day viewed this type of vehicle with favour. Certain regulations appertaining to driving licences, speeds and taxation were relaxed with regard to the road tractor so long as it came within certain limits, so about nine manufacturers were offering this type of vehicle.

After World War II the road tractor was again popular because of the shortage of motive units but as the country became more prosperous more orthodox vehicles became more widespread and the road tractor went into decline.

PRAGA
[68]

Plate 68 shows a vehicle from the Czechoslovakian factory of Praga, a name which goes back as far as 1910.

The vehicle depicted is a model V3S, an air cooled diesel 6 × 6 which is produced as a truck, tipper or tanker in standard form. The chassis has a mean wheelbase of 4,140 mm, overall length of 6,910 mm and is carried on 825 × 20 tyres.

Power is provided by the Praga T912 six-cylinder air cooled diesel engine of 110 mm bore and 130 mm stroke giving a cubic capacity of 7,412 cc. Output is 98 bhp at 2,100 rpm.

A four-speed gearbox is fitted to the vehicle but for maximum traction a super low or crawler gear is fitted, and together with the six-wheel drive layout of the vehicle this gives it considerable cross country abilities and makes it very useful for site work.

HENDRICKSON
[69]

The Hendrickson name goes back as far as 1914 when the Hendrickson Motor Truck Company was set up in Chicago. The one event that has made the name known in almost every vehicle building country of the world happened in 1926 when the firm produced its first truck embodying its own design of tandem axle suspension. Since that time the Company has become a specialist in rear bogie suspension systems for both tandems and tridems, and many other truck and trailer builders include Hendrickson-designed suspensions in their productions.

By the use of an equalizing beam to connect the two axles from below and a pair of semi-elliptic springs to provide the suspension, the two axles are held parallel to one another and the amount of rise in one axle is halved at the spring centre by the action of the beam. Above the axles torque rods are provided to take the braking and driving torque and relieve the road springs of this function.

In later designs the usual semi-elliptic steel leaf springs have been replaced by rubber load cushions, rubber air springs and rubber in shear for various uses. Forged aluminium beams are also used where weight saving is of prime importance.

As a custom builder Hendrickson produce all manner of designs. They include over-the-road tractors in coe and conventional form, truck mixer chassis, dumpers, off-highway tractors, dock shunters, heavy duty tractors and crane chassis. Four, six and eight-wheel chassis employing single, double and tridem axle drives, tag and pusher axles are all available from Hendrickson.

Plate 69 shows a four-axle dump operated by Wanatah Trucking Co Inc of Wanatah, Indiana. This truck is fitted with Hendrickson tandem drive on the last two axles while the second axle, ahead of the rear bogie, is fitted with Neway air suspension and air lift for use when running empty. Dump body and hoist are by Hercules Galion.

WE AND DIVCO
[70 and 71]

The Express Dairy Company of London started to experiment with mechanically propelled milk floats in 1932 when a small fleet of GV electrics were tried at branches in north London. Following the success of these first units the fleet was gradually added to and the horse-drawn vans withdrawn.

Many different types of electric trucks have been used during the period under review including Metrovick, Brush, NCB, Electricar, Morrison, Electruk and Wales and Edwards.

As rounds have increased so the weight to be carried has gone up and a truck with larger capacity has been sought. In 1964 a handful of articulated Wales and Edwards (WE) electrics were tried (Plate 70); these had a capacity of 30 cwts.

In some outlying areas the staying power of electrics was taxed to the limit of their batteries so small petrol and oil engined vehicles were used for this type of operation. Several small commercials in the 1 to $1\frac{1}{2}$-ton bracket were used including Commer, Austin, Morris Commerical and Trojan. One particularly unusual acquisition was an American Divco delivery van (Plate 71), and this was used in the Watford area for a while.

The Divco was a type which was specially designed for multiple stop delivery and the original design goes back to 1927. The model shown in the plate was powered by a four-cylinder 47 bhp petrol engine and the driver sat on a tip-up seat which allowed for easy entry and exit. The chassis was dropped in the centre so that there was only one step to the ground and over the rear wheels the floor was flat at a height of 2 ft 6 in.

NAZAR
[72]

There have been around twenty different Spanish makes of commercials extant during the period under review and quite a number of these have appeared since World War II.

In Spain, in common with other countries of Europe and the Far East, a number of small vans and three-wheelers have made an appearance. These include Avia, Biscuter, Derbi, Eucort, FH, Iresa, Isocarro, Mymsa, Roa, SEAT, Trimak, and Vespacar.

Regarding the heavier vehicles, the old Hispano Suiza name faded out just after the war, and in the years immediately following Babcock, Barreiros, Ebro, Karpetan, Nazar and Pegaso started producing vehicles, each taking a share of the market.

The Babcock was rather short-lived and the Karpetan probably also; the Barreiros became part of the Chrysler empire after a previous association with AEC, and Ebro started off as a Spanish assembly plant for British Ford chassis.

Pegaso is looked upon as being *the* Spanish commerical and a connection was made with Leyland early on by the use of Leyland 'Comet' running units for the four-wheel Pegaso chassis. The Pegaso concern had been established in 1946 by the acquisition of the old Hispano plant at Barcelona and, largely by finance raised by the Instituto Nacional de Industria, a second factory was established in Madrid.

Barreiros started in 1954 and became Chrysler Espana SA in 1970. Production has consisted of medium and heavyweight trucks, also buses and agricultural tractors. Since acquisition by Chrysler certain small vehicles imported from America are sold as Barreiros Dodge.

Plate 72 shows a Nazar truck of the 1960s. This is a model from the small range of 5½-, 7- and 9-ton capacity vehicles produced at that time. The Nazar factory started about 1958 in Zaragoza and assembled vehicles using Perkins and Henschel engines.

SR
[73]

The only heavy commercial vehicle currently produced in the Rumanian Peoples Republic is the SR produced at the Steagul Rosu factory at Brasov. Production commenced in 1964 and two main models are produced, the 'Bucegi' and the 'Carpati'.

Plate 73 shows a model from the Carpati range – which gets its name from the nearby Carpathian mountains. This is the 3-ton capacity model which is powered by a V8 petrol engine which produces 140 bhp at 3,600 rpm and is fitted with a four-speed gearbox.

The Bucegi range consists of both bonnetted and forward control models in sizes up to about 18 tons gross for a three-axle articulated type.

HANOMAG
[74]

One of the problems facing vehicle designers is that the loading height of a vehicle with a flat floor is directly related to the tyre size used. This is particularly important on local delivery vehicles where the driver is continually having to jump up onto the vehicle to get at the load and the ideal is for a floor level to be something less than a metre from the ground.

As the tyre size has a direct relation to the amount of weight that can be carried any reduction in tyre size brings about a lessening of payload unless the number of tyres can be increased. To add another axle is costly and it adds to the unladen weight of the vehicle.

Faced with problems of this sort the German Coca Cola concern came up with the design of low loading truck shown in Plate 74. This ultra-low loader is based on a light truck chassis with front wheel drive produced by Rheinstahl Hanomag, and it features double rear axles mounted on very small section tyres. With a payload of only $1\frac{1}{2}$ tons it is possible to use such small tyres, partly because of the fact that no drive line is required and minimum ground clearance is not impaired. The rear tyres carry weight only, the normal section front tyres are on the driving axle.

The Hanomag 'Kurier' chassis used for the vehicle was originally a production of Vidal und Sohn of Hamburg, a company which produced light vans under the name of Tempo from 1928 until 1963 when it passed to the control of Hanomag. Within a short while this concern became Hanomag Henschel and soon afterwards the lighter vehicle section of the Company was transferred to Mercedes Benz.

WHITE
[75]

The desirable qualities of an aircraft fueller are adequate capacity, high rate of pumping ability, low overall height and a high degree of manoeuvrability.

One design of fueller which goes a long way in satisfying these demands is the White model pictured in Plate 75. This is a vehicle specially designed for the purpose and not merely a conversion of a production chassis.

The vehicle is based on a twin steering chassis which gives good steering capabilities on three axles without the use of a rear bogie which promotes tyre scrubbing. The cab is positioned well forward and low down so as to give minimum overall height.

The space alongside the one-man cab is available for some of the pumping and metering equipment which is easily accessible to the driver. It is also well positioned for placing the vehicle close to under-wing fuelling points with least delay and risk of damage. Additional fuelling lines at the side of the truck are for use when an aircraft has fuel tanks located in other positions.

The 8,000 gallon tank was built by the Columbian Steel Tank Company and the engine is mounted in a special compartment at the rear of the vehicle.

MOWAG
[76 and 77]

Plate 77 shows a 1963 Mowag under-floor engined vehicle specially built for the transport of long lengths of steel beams, angles, tubes and rods. It is of integral construction with a chassis frame made up of welded angle forming the body floor as well as making a space frame for the running gear.

With a wheelbase of 4,500 mm and an overall length of 8,390 mm, the body is 6,600 mm long. Steel stock of much greater

156

length than the body can be carried without resorting to the use of heavy front and rear bolsters because a narrow cab leaves space on either side for long lengths of steel to project beyond the front of the vehicle. The two-seater cab is entered by a hinged door at the front.

The complete vehicle is given a low profile by mounting the cab low down at the front, and entry is by only one step. This is made possible by the adoption of an under-floor engine mounted below the chassis frame behind the front axle.

A flat opposed 8-cylinder SLM air cooled diesel engine is fitted. This is of 10.6 litres capacity and produces 150 bhp at 2,200 rpm. Drive is by means of a six-speed ZF gearbox to a two-speed rear axle.

To increase further the productivity of the design, a single axle trailer has been added. This trailer can be used to carry short lengths of steel or merely to support the rear end of long lengths of concrete reinforcing rods that are being carried (Plate 76).

FAR
[78]

Tractors FAR grew out of an organisation which marketed trailers built by Legache and Glaszmann during the 1920s. The original design of the tractors was very similar to the Chenard and Walcker light road tractor.

During the 1930s three-wheel tractors were produced under licence from the British Scammell firm – the early design of 'Mechanical Horse'. In the years after World War II the Scammell 'Scarab' was again built under licence but this time a flat fronted cab was used in place of the British Scammell rounded front type (Plate 78).

The heavier four-wheel tractor in the post-war range was based on Renault cab and running units, while a much heavier tractor was produced for French Railways for handling the trailers of the Kangerou type on and off railway wagons.

Latest type of tractor is a medium weight outfit of forward control design utilising certain Berliet running units and cab. The

157

vehicle embodies a new FAR designed automatic coupling gear which is controlled completely from the driver's cab. All brake pipes, electrical connections and landing gear movement is controlled by the driver without leaving the cab.

WILLEME
[79]

Established just after the 1914–1918 war when there were many American Liberty trucks in Europe, Willeme built up their business by producing these vehicles under licence as well as repairing and rebuilding the wartime types. Ever since that time the Willeme emblem has been a Liberty truck held high by the Statue of Liberty.

From the experience gained in the formative years of the company it was possible to introduce a larger version in 1927 and within a short while a rigid six-wheeler and articulated versions appeared.

A large part of Willeme production was taken up with building dump trucks, tippers, heavy haulage tractors, special vehicles designed for desert use, crane carriers and fire trucks. Two of the heaviest and best known models were the 70-ton payload six-wheel tractor design of 1939 and the 125-ton eight-wheeled bonnetted tractor produced in 1949 to work with a Scari trailer. The whole outfit was designed to gross 205 tons, and went to work in Portugal.

In the late 1950s an eight-wheeled 'Auto crane' was produced for the French Air Force and a series of powerful (330 hp) 6 × 6 airfield crash tenders entered service at airfields throughout France.

Great things were expected of the association between Willeme and the British AEC concern. Announced in May 1962 with a range covering a wide variety of types of both Willeme and AEC design, the joint venture did not make the inroads into the European market as hoped. A similar agreement was made with the British BMC concern with regard to the marketing of the lighter 'Willeme BMC' range, but both ventures lasted only about three years.

The death of the founder in the late 1960s did not help matters with the Willeme company and soon after this the Nanterre factory closed down. The stock of spare parts, drawings and unfinished chassis passed into the hands of Perez and Raimond who took up the fabrication of new vehicles – mostly 6 × 4 tippers for export – as well as the rebuilding of older chassis as required. They produced an 8 × 4 heavy haulage tractor design in 1973. Crane carrier chassis also form part of the production and in the same factory the PRP vehicle is produced in small numbers to special order.

Plate 79 shows one of the final Willeme designs, an LF model 4 × 2 tractor with NH type cab and Willeme engine, in this instance coupled to a short-wheelbase bulk powder trailer.

OSHKOSH
[80]

Oshkosh Motor Truck Inc of Oshkosh, Wisconsin was founded just after World War I and started by producing light trucks in the 1-ton to 3-ton range. Over the years the range has been extended upwards and today Oshkosh produce mainly tractors and trucks at the heavy end of the scale.

One of the largest productions has been the special tractor shown in Plate 80. This is an 8 × 8 tractor for hauling up to 125 tons, built for the Bigge Drayage Co of San Leandro, California.

The massive tractor, designated model 88-H-3655, was built specially for the operator in collaboration with Peerless Trailer and Truck Service of Portland, Oregon who supplied the low bed trailer.

Power for the outfit is supplied by a Caterpillar 1693 six-cylinder diesel which produces 375 bhp at 2,000 rpm from its 893 cu in. capacity. A Twin-Disc torque converter and automatic transmission are fitted in order to reduce transmission shocks through normal gear changing.

Although it weighs 32,000 lbs the tractor is capable of up to 50 mph on the road. A 30,000 lb capacity winch is mounted between the cab and the fifth wheel for use when heavy loads have to be winched and jacked into position.

The Peerless trailer has a rated capacity of 80 tons, is carried on 60 Michelin tyres and has its own Continental engine at the rear which powers the hydraulic pumps for varying the height of the trailer bed from ground level to 2 ft off the road surface. Overall the complete outfit measures 112 ft.

BUSSING
[81]

A type of vehicle which shows original thought is the Bussing Decklaster which was produced by the German company and first shown by them at the 1965 Frankfurt Show (Plate 81).

The basis of the design is a truck which can carry small palletised containers, be loaded and unloaded from either end, be capable of loading from either bank or ground level, and yet be completely self-contained so that work can be carried out at remote points.

It will be seen from the illustration that these basic requirements have been met by carrying the containers on two sets of rails which run along the complete length of the vehicle so that loading/unloading can take place from either end. The movement of the containers whilst on the vehicle is carried out mechanically. The rails are mounted at a height of 1.5 m from the ground to match the height of the loading bank. Should there be a slight variation in the vehicle height because of loading conditions, then the vehicle's height can be varied by the air bag suspension. For ground level loading a pedestrian-controlled fork lift truck is carried at the rear of the vehicle and the batteries on this can be charged whilst the vehicle is moving.

It will be noted that the cab of the vehicle has had to be positioned low down at the front in order to accommodate the end to end load carrying portion. The floor rails project beyond the cab to locate with those on the loading bank.

Because of the position of the cab the engine has had to be mounted under the chassis behind the second axle – a position much used by Bussing. A twin-steering front axle layout has been used to enable a full 15-ton load to be carried without resorting to the more usual, but heavier, tandem rear axles.

JAY-FONG
[82]

In Plate 82 is illustrated a 4-ton capacity truck from China, the Jay-Fong CA 10Z. Readers will no doubt think that the shape of this truck is familiar, and in fact the vehicle, like the Russian ZIL-585 and KAZ-600, is modelled on the International Harvester K series of the World War II period. Many thousands of American vehicles were shipped to Asia during the war as part of the Lend-Lease scheme and some of the designs have been perpetuated until quite recently.

The particular type shown was marketed by the China National Machinery Import and Export Corporation and follows the general lines of a dropside lorry for use over unmade country if required.

A brief specification of the vehicle is:
Wheelbase: 4,000 mm
Overall length: 6,600 mm
Overall width: 2,460 mm
Overall height: 2,200 mm
Unladen weight: 3,800 kg
Gross vehicle weight: 8,025 kg
Engine: Six-cylinder petrol engine
  Bore: 101.6 mm, stroke: 114.3 mm
  Output: 95 bhp at 2,800 rpm
Clutch: Twin dry plate
Gearbox: Five-speed
Rear axle: Double reduction type
Tyre size: 900 × 20
Turning circle: 8.6 m

ATKINSON
[83]

The name Atkinson was first connected with vehicles during the period 1907 to 1933 when the Atkinson Walker steam wagons were being produced. As the sales of steamers dwindled because of legislative restrictions and the steady progress of the internal combustion engine, Atkinson turned to the conversion of lorries to diesel power and the adding of extra axles.

Atkinson Lorries (1933) Ltd was formed and the first diesel powered lorries soon appeared. Most of the production since that time has centred on lorries although a few buses and crane carrier chassis have been built at times.

In 1966 there appeared a pair of Atkinson tractors which, as far as Britain was concerned, were unique, being twin steer tractors with a load carrying portion added between the cab and the fifth wheel.

Based on special 'Silver Knight' chassis with 13 ft wheelbase, the tractors were acquired for use with Boden tandem axle semi-trailers. The resulting five axle combinations carried three spherical pressure vessels by Interconsult for the transport of salt in bulk. One of these tanks was carried on the tractor between the cab and the fifth wheel coupling and two were mounted on the trailer chassis together with a separate engine to supply power for blower discharge of the load into overhead silos. The unladen weight of the outfit was 11 tons 19 cwt and it operated at 32 tons gross (Plate 83).

J Spurling Ltd, a member of Transport Development Group operated the vehicles on hire to ICI Ltd, and the operation schedule was that the vehicles collected 19½ tons of salt from Stoke Prior, Bromsgrove each night and return to London. The tractor unit was uncoupled and used as a rigid vehicle whilst an orthodox tractor was coupled to the trailer portion and it was used as a separate vehicle for deliveries to other customers in the London area.

TERMINAL TUG
[84]

The Terminal Tug shown in Plates 84a and 84b is a shunting tractor specially designed for use in terminal yards, docks, industrial yards and freight depots. It is produced by Bulk Transport Systems of the FMC Corporation and is aimed at operators who need a tractor capable of handling both normal semi-trailers and full drawbar trailers in the confines of their yards or depots.

The basic design consists of a 10 ft 5 in.-wheelbase tractor with an overall length of 18 ft 1 in. Powered by a GM V6 petrol engine rated at 157 bhp, the drive is taken through an Allison Torqmatic transmission system to an Eaton double reduction axle located under the fifth wheel coupling.

At the extreme rear of the chassis is fitted the 'auto-dolly' coupling for hitching up drawbar trailers or the dolly of a 'doubles' outfit. This coupler is hydraulically controlled and is capable of engaging a drawbar eye at heights ranging from 8 in. to 45 in. from the ground. Like the hydraulically elevated fifth wheel coupling the 'auto-dolly' can be controlled from the driver's cab.

The cab itself is an interesting feature because of its ability to be turned through 90 degrees to give the driver a better view down the sides of trailers when handling them in confined spaces. All controls including coupling, locking and raising are carried out from within the cab. The only function which requires the driver to leave his cab is the handling of the air brake pipes.

SISU
[85]

The Sisu concern has its beginnings in 1931 when Tor Nessling, a young Finnish engineer, took to building the first home produced truck. Success did not come overnight, but gradually orders were taken and twelve were produced during the first year. During the 1930s production gradually expanded and the first exports were made to neighbouring countries.

Wartime production centred around trucks for the Finnish army, and at the end of hostilities expansion of the range got under way. It was later to embrace buses, fire engines and cross-country vehicles as well as railway rolling stock. Because of the country's natural terrain and industry, logging vehicles have always been well to the fore in output. As this and other home industries have expanded so the need for vehicles has grown in numbers as well as in the size of load to be handled. Many heavy tractors, tippers and dumpers have been produced to handle movements of machinery and the transport of quarried materials.

Plate 85 shows a 1966 model K149 6 × 4 heavy haulage tractor for gross combination weights of up to 70,000 kg.

VANAJA
[86]

The Vanaja was rather short-lived, as production started just after World War II and finished in 1967.

At the end of World War II Vanaja was created out of the Sisu concern which had itself been created out of a fusion of two companies at the outbreak of war in order to concentrate production facilities.

A great part of the Company's production was in the field of 4 × 4 and 6 × 4 types because of the road and weather conditions prevailing in Finland which demand maximum traction.

During the 1960s a trading agreement was made with the British AEC concern for the supply of engines, axles and certain other running units, and many of the road tractors and logging outfits appeared with these proprietary items as standard fitments. After the merger of AEC and Leyland the Ergomatic tilt cab was used for the road tractors.

Plate 86 shows a 6 × 4 heavy haulage tractor of the early 1960s hauling a large steam boiler with a gross combination weight of 60 tons. The tractor is powered by an AEC AVT 690 turbocharged six-cylinder engine which drives through a Fuller RTO915 10-speed gearbox.

STAR
[87]

So far as I have been able to establish, during the period under review in this volume production of commercial vehicles in Poland has fallen within two broad categories – those produced

164

up to the early 1930s, and those built since World War II. During the late 1920s to early thirties there existed the AS light van produced by the Budowe Samochodow AS in Warsaw, and the Ursus lorry built by Zaklady Mechaniczne Ursus Spolka Akcyjna at Czechowice, Warsaw.

Postwar production has of course been more organised into the country's planned programme for the expansion of engineering with exports being made to other States. The Star 20 lorry was the first model and this series emanates from the Fabryka Samochodow Ciezarowych at Starachowice which continues to produce later models of the type. The factory at Lublin builds the Zuk light van, while the Nysa is made at the Zaklady Budowy Nadwozi Samochodowich in the town of the same name. At the Jelkzanskie Samochodow Ciezarowych at Jelcz k/Olawy the Jelcz, at one time called the Zubr, is produced, and at the factory in Warsaw a van version of the Warszawa car is made.

Zuk and Nysa vehicles use components from the Warszawa car – engine, rear axle, suspension and steering gear. The Zuk is a 900-kg capacity truck or van with four-cylinder 70 hp engine, and the Nysa is a 880-kg van. An alternative 1500-cc engine of Fiat design is used for the larger load-carrying Zuk models, and fire engine, dropside truck, van and tilt van body styles are available. Nysa delivery vans were first introduced in 1968 and were quickly followed by minibus, ambulance and refrigerated van body styles. This vehicle is powered by a four-cylinder 2,120 cc petrol engine developing 77 bhp at 4,000 rpm.

The most popular Star types are models 28 and 29, which differ only in the type of engine. The 28 has the S-530A six-cylinder 105 $\times$ 120 diesel engine while the 29 has a petrol engine of 105 bhp output from its six cylinders of 95 $\times$ 110. Payload of the Star is stated to be 5,000 kg solo or about 9,280 kg gross. A trailer can be towed and then the gross train weight is stated to be 14,530 kg. Wheelbase is 3,400 mm, overall length 6,430 mm, tyre size 8.25 $\times$ 20. The cab is of French Chausson design.

A cross country three-axle Star is also produced, the 660 (Plate 87). This is available with either petrol or oil engine, is of all wheel drive pattern and is carried on 12.00 $\times$ 18 tyres. The Star 200 is the latest addition to the range and is a 6-ton load carrier.

Three models are produced under the Jelcz title: the 315, 316 and 317.

The Jelcz 315 is a forward control truck designed for a payload of 8,000 kg (15,045 kg gvw) or about 18,000 kg (29,000 kg

165

gtw) with a trailer. It is powered by the SW680/1 diesel engine, which is a six-cylinder unit built under Leyland licence, and power is taken through a single plate clutch and five-speed gearbox to a double reduction rear axle.

The Jelcz 316 is a 6 × 2 model for loads of 11,000 kg solo, while the 317 is a tractor model built to operate at 28,000 kg gross combined weight with a tandem axle semi-trailer.

ISCO
[88, 89, 90, 91, 92 and 93]

In order to show the wide diversity of equipment produced by a small volume specialist vehicle builder a random selection from the Isco range is shown in Plates 89 to 93.

Isco took over the old Cline truck building company which was started in the 1950s and produced highway tractors, oilfield trucks, mixers, dumpers and heavy duty tractors for construction work.

Present production includes normal and bottom dumps, crane trucks, logging tractors and special vehicles for railway operation such as cranes, shunters and lifting equipment, both with and without railway running gear.

Plate 90 shows a 60-ton steel mill slag hauling unit, Plate 92 a 5-SW model 'Shuttle Wagon' or railway yard shunter equipped for handling van semi-trailers and Plate 93 shows a railway shunting engine capable of handling up to five loaded box cars by means of Ryd-A-Rail flanged wheel attachment. Plate 91 depicts a conventional stake truck converted to operate on railway tracks by means of the hydraulically operated Ryd-A-Rail adaptation, while in Plate 89 is shown a IC-A22-R articulated rear dump with 16.5 cu yd body.

As mentioned above Isco Manufacturing Company of Kansas City took over the old Cline truck line and one of the earlier heavy duty tractors is shown in Plate 88.

SICARD
[94]

Although they are concerned mainly with snow clearance vehicles, refuse disposal vehicles and crane carrier chassis, Sicard have in the past also produced over-the-road tractors and six-wheel dumpers.

Originally FWD chassis were used and more recently components from Chrysler, Cummins, Detroit Diesel, Waukesha, Continental, International, Clark, Timken, Lipe Rollway and KW-Dart have been employed.

Plate 94 shows a typical Sicard product in the shape of the 'Snowmaster', which is busy clearing an airfield runway. In conditions such as this it is usual for a series of these machines to work as a team, each sweeping a path and ejecting the snow up to 200 ft to one side in order to make the surface suitable for use by aircraft once more.

This model, the 'Snowmaster BL' operates at a gross vehicle weight of 35,000 lbs. All-wheel traction is used and either petrol or diesel engines are available. The standard power unit for the blower, as opposed to the propelling engine, is an Allis Chalmers 21,000 six-cylinder diesel engine of 844 cu in. displacement which produces 340 bhp at 2000 rpm.

WALTER
[95, 96, 97, 98 and 99]

The first Walter car appeared in 1898 from a factory on West 65th Street, Manhattan. By 1905 production was up to 300 a

167

year, most of the parts being made in the Company's own plant. 1906 saw the formation of the Walter Auto Company, but by 1911 it was decided to concentrate on truck production and the Walter Motor Truck Company was created with a plant at Queens, Long Island. From 1957 the factory has been at Voorheesville, NY.

For a great part of its life Walter has produced normal trucks as well as the famous snow ploughs, fire engines and other special vehicles. In recent years the Company has concentrated on producing a custom built 4 × 4 chassis for special purposes, featuring Walter four point positive drive and 100 per cent traction. A feature of the Walter is that there is no transfer case as such, the drive being taken from the engine to the gearbox and then by straight shafts to front and rear axle drive shafts. The bevel gears, differentials and brakes are all inboard within the frame and the final reduction is achieved by employing internal ring gears inside the wheels. As the drive shafts are separated from the axles proper it is possible to utilise the solid forged steel front axle to mount the plough in the snowplough tractor.

Plate 95 shows a Walter wing type snowplough, 96 an aircraft towing tractor and 97 a rotary type snow blower. Plate 98 depicts a front wheel drive low loading truck and Plate 99 is an airfield crash tender.

CSEPEL
[100]

Commercial vehicles produced in Hungary are distributed by the Mogurt Trading Company. The Csepel illustrated in Plate 100 is one of the models available which are built at the Csepel Engineering Works near Budapest. Production of vehicles began in 1950 with models based on Steyr designs.

During the 1960s production included the D450 range of bonnetted four-wheelers powered by the D414 four-cylinder diesel engine of 5517cc capacity (112 mm bore and 140 mm stroke), which produced 100 bhp at 2,300 rpm. Drive was through a single dry plate clutch and five-speed gearbox to a spiral bevel rear axle.

A six-cylinder version of the above engine was used to power the forward control models D510, D707 and D710. This engine produced 145 bhp at 2,300 rpm from its 8,275 cc capacity; a similar five-speed gearbox was fitted.

In 1972 two new models were produced: the D453 and the D730. Both are four-wheel forward control models, the former using the D414 engine while the latter uses the D614 six-cylinder unit of 8,275 cc.

The D453 is based on the Polish Star 642 model while the D730 is modelled after the Jelcz 113, also from Poland.

Plate 100 gives elevations of a Model D344 of 1963. This 4 × 4 truck is powered by the 4-cylinder D414h oil engine mentioned above. It has a five-speed gearbox and is carried on 900 × 20 tyres.

USSR
[101, 102, 103, 104, 105, 106, 107, 108 and 109]

Prior to the Revolution there were four small works engaged in building motor vehicles in Russia, the AMO factory, the Ruskii Renault, the Russko-Baltiisky and the Lebedev.

1 November 1924 saw the first truck produced in the AMO Moscow factory. This was the AMO-F-15, a small four-wheel truck with a capacity of 1,500 kg and weighing 1,920 kg unladen. A four-cylinder 4,400 cc engine of 35 bhp propelled the vehicle at speeds up to 35 kph. By March 1925 production had risen to one vehicle per day, and the model continued until 1931.

The Yaraslavl works was opened in 1925, and in 1927 it was decided to reconstruct the AMO works. At this time work began on another new works, this time at Gorky. By 1928 truck production has reached a figure of 790 a year.

When the rebuilding of the old AMO works was completed it

was decided to rename the factory as a tribute to the leader Joseph Stalin, so from 1 October 1931 the works became known as Zavod Imeny Stalin or ZIS. Soon after, in January 1932 the new Gorky works got under way with the production of the GAZ-AA type which was based on the Ford Model A of the period. This was the start of the Russki-Ford which later embraced other models such as six-wheelers, pick-ups, ambulances and small buses. Production of the GAZ-AAA (the six-wheeler) finished in 1945 while the GAZ-AA four-wheeler continued until 1948.

The Yaraslavl works produced the first six-wheeler in 1932 – the YAG or JAG 10 which was a 6 × 4 with 6-cylinder 60 bhp engine of 4,880 cc capacity. Payload was 8,000 kg and unladen weight 5,430 kg. This was swiftly followed by an 8 × 4 version which was certainly unusual, as it was of normal control (bonnetted) layout. Produced from 1932 to 1941, this vehicle had a payload of 12,000 kg and was propelled by a six-cylinder engine of 7,020 cc.

The ZIS range continued with 4 × 2, 6 × 4 and 4 × 4 models and a halftrack appeared in 1938. This factory also produced vehicles built from parts supplied by the Ural works which had been built at Miass during 1942/43 following the German advance deep into Russia. In 1944 the Ural works started to produce their own range of vehicles and the first model was a 3-tonner.

Most of the wartime vehicle production centred around a 1½-tonner produced at the GAZ works and the ʼ3-ton ZIS, but of course large numbers of American trucks were imported under the Lend-Lease agreements.

Postwar demands for commercial vehicles meant new factories had to be built and in 1947 the Minsk works was opened with a 6/7-tonner as its first model. In 1951 another works was opened at Kutaisi where the ZIS-150 was the first type produced, and shortly afterwards a plant at Ulyanovsk opened for the production of the GAZ-69 cross country truck.

In 1956 a change was made at the ZIS factory. In future it was to be known as ZIL in commemoration of a former factory director, Likachev.

1959 saw the opening of two further plants for vehicle production. One at Kremenchug started by producing the Kraz 10/12-ton dump truck and the Kraz 12/14-ton general haulage vehicle, while the plant in Byelorussia was built to produce Belaz dump trucks of 25 and 40 ton capacity.

By 1968 production of Russian vehicles had reached 800,000 per year, and in 1971 truck production alone was 609,000 units. Similarly export figures had risen at a tremendous rate: during the period 1949–1959 some 31,600 trucks were exported, and during the period 1960–1968 the figure had risen to 216,000.

Latest developments are the production of even larger dump trucks of up to 120 tons capacity for work at opencast coal mines and quarries, and new designs for freight chassis including tippers, articulated units and haulage vehicles for trailer operation.

The large capacity articulated dumper to be built at the Belaz works in Byelorussia features a gas turbine power plant, while the more normal freight chassis are to be built at the new Kamaz plant. This new factory is almost a new town in itself for the area covered is in the region of 100 sq km and includes foundry, forge, press-shop, engine, wheel and assembly plants. This latest and largest automobile works is situated at Naberezhynie Chelny on the banks of the Kama river and an annual output of 150,000 units is planned. The range of vehicles will include a 16-ton lorry and trailer outfit, a 20-ton tractor unit and a three-axle tipper.

The first few experimental chassis were produced at the ZIL works and the bodies were the product of the Belaz plant. Extensive trials took place in the Moscow area prior to the works going into full scale production.

Currently, production in Russia covers a wide range of vehicles including the following:

GAZ 53A: a four-wheel NC sided vehicle for 4,000 kg loads

GAZ 66: 4 × 4 and trailer with V8 92 mm × 80 mm engine of 115 bhp

MAZ 500A: four-wheel FC sided truck of 9-ton capacity

MAZ 503A: four-wheel FC tipper

MAZ 504A: four-wheel FC tractor unit

MAZ 516: six-wheel FC sided truck with V6 diesel of 210 bhp

KRAZ 255B: bonnetted 6 × 6 cross-country truck

KRAZ 256B: bonnetted 6 × 4 tipper

KRAZ 257: bonnetted 6 × 4 for trailer operation

KRAZ 258: 30-ton 6 × 4 tractor with V8 diesel of 265 bhp

URAL 375: 5-ton 6 × 6 cross-country truck

URAL 377: 7½-ton 6 × 4 cross-country truck

ZIL 130V1: four-wheel NC tractor

ZIL 130G: four-wheel sided truck

ZIL 130B1: four-wheel NC tractor unit

ZIL 555: four-wheel tipper

ZIL 131: 6 × 6 truck with V8 petrol engine
BELAZ 540: 25-ton dump truck
BELAZ 548: 40-ton dump truck

MOL
[110]

The Mol company was started by Mr Gerard Mol just after the end of World War II. With so many ex-military vehicles around the business of rebuilding used trucks was carried on together with bodywork construction and trailer building.

In recent years production has expanded to include complete vehicles of a specialist nature. Current models include TIR style semi-trailers, trailers equipped for the French Kangerou system, low loading trailers with detachable gooseneck, tankers, tippers, truckmixers, 4 × 4 vehicles for desert use, 4 × 4 and 6 × 6 trucks for oilfields, 6 × 4 tippers and a wide variety of crane carrier chassis including 6 × 4 ,6 × 6, 8 × 6 and 10 × 6 types. A heavy haulage tractor has also been built which utilises a 12 × 6 layout and can handle 80-ton loads.

In Plate 110 is shown a 6 × 6 tipper of the mid 1960s period when a cab and front end of Magirus Deutz style was being used. Most Mol vehicles have Deutz air cooled diesel engines installed as standard.

KALMAR
[111]

The Daf Variomatic automatic belt transmission system is an example of an unusual design which has proved most successful in a variety of applications. This system is produced by Van Doorne of Eindhoven, Holland for use in their range of light cars and

172

vans, and in recent years it has been taken up by manufacturers in other countries.

One such application is the Kalmar small van which was first produced in 1965 by Kalmar Verkstads Ab for the Swedish Post Office. The specification includes the Daf 750-cc engine, variomatic transmission, wheels and suspension, and with an unladen weight of 850 kg, a payload of 400 kg is obtained. After extensive trials of 10 vans lasting over two years the Swedish Post Office placed an order for 1,000 such vans (Plate 111).

An indication of the versatility of the Daf belt drive Variomatic system is its adoption by various producers for differing tasks. The United States Army has found use for the system in the Pony, a small 4 × 4 cross country vehicle which uses the flat 500 cc 2-cylinder power unit. With a tare weight of approximately 500 kg the Pony is designed to take a load of about the same weight and has a permanently engaged four wheel drive for better traction over difficult terrain.

Another firm to adopt the Daf variomatic system is the Arkansas Gas Company of America which required 100 small pickups but rejected the usual Daf design because of the body size. By fabricating their own design of body and cab around the Daf engine, transmission and other running units the Gas Company have created a fleet of ¾-ton pick-ups to their liking.

Although it is only a one-off vehicle, another application of the Daf system is a Norwegian design for a motor sleigh with skis at the front and tracks at the rear.

HOLDEN
[112]

Produced by General Motors Holden in Australia is the Belmont panel van illustrated in Plate 112. A pick-up version of the vehicle is called the Kingswood and both are offered with a choice of engines.

Obviously based on contemporary American car and pick-up practice, the Holden van and pick-up provide swift transport for the shopkeeper, contractor or private owner. The 111-in. wheelbase vehicle measures 184.8 in. overall and is 71.8 in. wide. A choice of no less than five engine options is offered, made up of two different capacity straight sizes and two V types. These are the 161, a 114 bhp six-cylinder of 3.375 in. × 3 in., the 186, a 130 bhp six of 3.625 in. × 3 in., the 186s, a 145 bhp rating of the 186, the 253, a 3.625 in. × 3.062 in. V8 and the 307, which is another V8 of 3.875 in. × 3.25 in.

The Belmont van has a capacity of 105 cu ft while the Kingswood pickup has a load space of 80.6 in. × 57.8 in. with 16.7in. high sides. The vehicle is also available in chassis/cab form for certain varieties of body style, and a 1-ton capacity model was introduced in 1971.

FAUN
[114]

Fahrzeugwerke Ansbach und Nurnburg was set up in 1916 and both private cars and commercial vehicles were produced until the mid 1920s when it was decided to concentrate on commercials.

In addition to orthodox lorries powered by petrol, oil and electricity, FAUN have built many types of specialist vehicles including road tractors, crane carriers, dumpers, slag haulers, road/rail vehicles, military and municipal.

Like Miesse in Belgium, FAUN tried their hand at producing a rigid eight-wheeler chassis during the 1930s but unlike Britain which took to the 'eight legger' this type of vehicle did not find a following in continental Europe.

Plate 114 shows a FAUN heavy haulage tractor of the 1970s, a model F610/36ZAN which is designed for trailed loads up to 80 tonnes. Other heavy haulage tractors in the range include 4 × 4s for loads of 40, 50, 60, 70 and 90 metric tons and a 4 × 2 for 30 tons. Six-wheel tractors in the range are designed for loads up to 100 metric tons.

Tippers in the range extend from 4 × 2s for 8 tons up to an 8 × 6 model for 17 tons payload, and 4 × 2 and 4 × 4 dumpers have capacities ranging from 11 to 80 tons.

Other special vehicles include four-, six- and eight-wheeled slag carriers and a range of airfield crash tenders up to 8 × 8 configuration. Municipal sweepers and refuse vehicles are also produced together with a range of articulated heavy haulage tractors up to an 8 × 6 model, while the crane carrier chassis include 4 × 4, 6 × 4, 6 × 6, 8 × 4, 8 × 6, 10 × 4, 10 × 6 and 10 × 8 models.

AUTOCAR
[115]

No doubt impressed by the performance of ex-military vehicles, several European operators of heavy transport equipment still continue to specify American chassis for their fleets, long after the war.

One such operator is Transports Jonet of Charleroi in southern Belgium who have several Autocars for heavy haulage tasks as well as the two Kenworths (Plate 59) and a Federal wrecker in their fleet.

Another transport specialist a little further north on the out-skirts of Bruxelles is Sogetra, a large construction company operating a fleet of dumpers, scrapers and ancillary vehicles on road construction work in Belgium. As well as the Autocar DC 7564T articulated dumps shown in Plate 114 the fleet includes DC 9364B six-wheel dumpers and mixers, Diamond T mixers and IHC dumps.

The DC 7564T double drive tractor is designed to operate at 100,000 lbs gross load on good roads. It is powered by the Cummins NH220 straight six-cylinder diesel of $5\frac{1}{8}$ in. × 6 in. (743 cu in.) which produces 220 bhp at the governed speed of 2,100 rpm. Drive is by way of a two plate dry clutch and 10-speed gearbox to a hypoid drive rear bogie.

The Fruehauf dump trailer coupled to the tractor in Plate 114 is carried on a tandem axle frame for stability in site work and is used to transport quarried materials for the foundations of Belgium's motorway network.

175

RALPH
[116]

Ralph trucks were the brainchild of Ralph Lewis, who started by building the first in borrowed premises with the aid of a friend, one mechanic and one labourer. This was in 1967, and with the aid of some financial backing Rolway Enterprises (Pty) Ltd was set up in Alberton, South Africa. This was really the only true truck so far produced in South Africa.

Based on current American practice, the Ralph was available in both cab-over and bonnetted versions, and supplied with either Cummins or GM V-configuration two-stroke CI engines. The smallest used the Cummins 270 engine while the largest, which was supplied to Consolidated Diamond Mines used the Cummins V-12 (V 1710-C) 525 bhp diesel.

Much other American equipment was used in the trucks including Jacobs engine brake, Kysor radiator shutters and air conditioning units. The vehicles also looked very American with their vertical exhaust stacks and chrome fuel tanks and fittings.

During the short life of the company a total of 42 trucks were turned out and they were well received by the South African press. Production ceased in the summer of 1971. Plate 116 shows one of the conventional tandems with the GM 8-V-71 Detroit Diesel installed driving through a 16 speed Spicer gearbox to RS rear axles.

HENSCHEL
[118]

In Germany during the 1960s there was a gradual swing away from the lorry and trailer concept toward the articulated type of vehicle for long distance transport. As the demand for greater payloads per single unit became more prevalent so the five axle 38-tonne artic loomed greater.

The five axle configuration was tackled in several ways and each design had its drawbacks:

1 four-wheel tractor with tri-axle semi-trailer
2 six-wheel tractor with tandem axle semi-trailer
3 twin steer six-wheel tractor with tandem axle semi-trailer
4 double drive six-wheel tractor with tandem axle semi-trailer
5 six-wheel tractor with twin steering and double drive coupled to tandem axle semi-trailer

The easiest system was 1, but this layout had the disadvantage of tyre scrubbing on the trailer tyres unless self steering axles were adopted.

Layout 2 was reasonable but there were penalties with regard to higher tractor weight and only single axle drive as in 1.

In 3 a lighter design of tractor was possible but as gross weights increased so the possibility of lost adhesion on a single drive was more likely.

Design 4 overcomes the drawback of lost adhesion mentioned above but a penalty of increased unladen weight is gained.

Layout 5 comes nearest to the ideal, having two steering axles for sure-footedness in bad conditions, a double drive to increase adhesion and slightly less unladen weight because of second axle design. However it is somewhat costly to produce an axle which both drives and steers and extremely so for one of this size.

Plate 118 shows the design of Henschel tractor which is of the type as outlined in 5 above. It is the model F221S-2AmS, a 3,610 mm wheelbase tractor with 240 bhp six-cylinder diesel engine.

HAYES
[119]

The Hayes-Anderson Motor Company Ltd was formed in 1922 and opened with a plant at Vancouver, Ontario. The reason for the start of the Company was that a need was seen for a truck that could withstand the strains of logging in the forests of British Columbia.

The production of heavy duty units progressed, and in 1928 a move was made to better premises in Vancouver and the name was changed to Hayes Manufacturing Company Ltd. Lighter trucks, fire engines, buses and railway carriages were produced for a while but the chief line was to remain the heavy logging outfits.

A notable model in the Hayes range of logging tractors was the HDX1000 series, one of which is shown in Plate 119. These mighty tractors are custom built and can be supplied with many options to the standard specification which is:

Frame: Hayes, fabricated from $16\frac{1}{2}$ in. × 7 in. I-beam structural steel

Front axle: Shuler 20,000 lb capacity

Rear axles: Rockwell Standard SFD 4640

Engine: Cummins NTC 335 diesel

Clutch: Spicer 2 plate dry

Transmission: Spicer

Tyre size: 12.00 × 24 and 14.00 × 24

The cab is offset to the left and the logging bolster has tyres of similar size to these of the tractor. Brakes are water cooled with a 400-gallon water tank and filters carried on the tractor. For empty running the bolster can be winched up on to the bolster of the tractor.

For less rigorous duties the 'Clipper' range includes conventional and coe models of straight truck and tractor types for line haul, dumper, oil field, logging, etc, with two- or three-axle layout.

PETERBILT
[120]

The Peterbilt Motors Company was established in 1939 by T A Peterman who purchased the old Fageol Truck and Coach factory at Oakland, California.

Since its inception Peterbilt has sought to produce trucks and tractors designed for the arduous conditions prevailing in the western states and logging outfits, dumpers and over-the-road tractors have been the mainstay of the output.

In 1960 Peterbilt moved to a new 33-acre site at Newark, California and this gave the company the room for expansion much needed at that time. To capture a share of the market in a different area of the United States an additional plant at Nashville, Tennessee was opened in 1969.

The first trucks were conventionals of two- and three-axle layout but in 1952 the first coe was produced, the model 350, and this type lasted until 1969.

An expansion of the range has taken place recently by the introduction of a middleweight series called the CB model. This was announced in 1971 and these cab forward models are produced to operate at 31,000 lbs and 47,000 lbs respectively.

Shown in Plate 120 is a model 351A operated by JDS Inc of Auburn, California with a bottom dump Fruehauf trailer for roadstone and aggregate hauling. This long-wheelbase model tractor has an extruded aluminium alloy chassis frame with aluminium crossmembers for lightness and as with all Peterbilt trucks the frame is of bolted construction.

The Model 351 is powered by a Cummins NTC-350 diesel engine of 855 cu in. displacement which produces 350 bhp at 2,100 rpm. The power is transmitted through a Dana-Spicer 2 plate clutch, Fuller RTO 9513 13 speed overdrive gearbox to a Rockwell Standard hypoid rear bogie.

VOLVO
[121]

Builders of trucks since 1928, Volvo have emerged as one of the principal heavy truck builders of Europe with exports going to 70 countries and as far away as Australia, where the first Volvo rigid eight-wheel chassis was produced in 1972 at the assembly plant there.

It was during the mid 1950s that Volvo really made headway in building trucks for the international fleets of northern Europe. Their turbo-charged diesel engine was said to add an extra 35 bhp to the 150 bhp output of the six-cylinder power unit with normal air intake. During this period the range consisted of the the L375, L385 and L395 types, all bonnetted models of four- and six-wheel layout. A 4 × 4 of similar general layout was the L38545.

During the 1960s the range was improved by the introduction of the L475, L485 and L495. Later in the sixties the F86, F88, FB88, N88 and NB88 series was introduced which set new standards for Volvo and resulted in many more sales in Europe and elsewhere.

The 1970s saw the introduction of the G88 with the TD100 250 bhp engine and the G89 powered by the TD120 330 bhp engine which goes under the title of '89 turbo 6'.

Plate 121 shows a 1972 Volvo FB88 6 × 4 tractor employed by Air Fina for the fuelling of jumbo jet aircraft at Bruxelles Airport. This tractor is fitted with the TD100 engine which drives through an eight-speed dual range gearbox to a Hendrickson rear bogie.

The tri-axle tank trailer is by Viberti of Italy and carries 80,000 litres of jet engine fuel which is delivered to the aircraft by way of two Vickers pumps.

The complete outfit weighs over 32 tonnes unladen while the combined gross weight is 96.18 tonnes. Overall length is 18.25 m, height 3.6 m and width 3.1 m.

INTERNATIONAL
[122]

In Plate 122 is shown what is believed to be the largest single unit petroleum tanker in the United States, a real 'Michigan Special'. Of all American states, which have a variety of sometimes complex regulations affecting the overall dimensions and weights of trucks, Michigan is looked upon by operators as the most favourable. Michigan has no regulation limiting gross vehicle weight as such, but does have laws which place a maximum on axle weights and inter-axle spacing.

By studying the regulations in detail the Kingsbury Oil Company Inc of Alpena in collaboration with International Harvester Co and Fruehauf Corporation have produced the articulated tanker shown which has a gross weight of 76 tons with a 52-ton payload!

Measuring 55 ft long the four compartment tank is 47 ft 2½ in. in length and carries 17,000 gallons. The tractor is a double drive C-OF 4090A model with 142-in. wheelbase and 434 bhp diesel engine.

The liberal Michigan laws apply only to those trucks operating within the State so the heavyweight outfit spends its time hauling petroleum products for the Atlantic Richfield Co. (ARCO) from their base at Bay City to the five bulk plants of Kingsbury Oil located in the north-east part of the state.

INDEX OF MANUFACTURERS

Numbers in bold type refer to colour illustrations.
Numbers in Roman type refer to pages.